MW01623940

Magic Lantern Guides
Proof of Purchase
Nikon SB-28
AF Speedlight

Magic Lantern Guides

Nikon SB-28

AF Speedlight

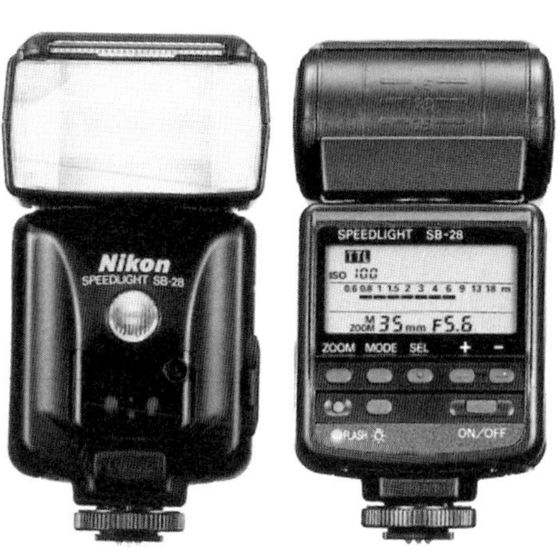

Michael Huber

Magic Lantern Guide to
Nikon SB-28 AF Speedlight

A Laterna magica® book

Published in the United States of America by

Silver Pixel Press®
A Tiffen® Company
21 Jet View Drive
Rochester, NY 14624

From the German edition by Michael Huber
Edited by Tony Munday
Translated by Phyllis M. Riefler-Bonham
Printed in Germany by Kösel GmbH, Kempten

Library of Congress Cataloging-in-Publication Data
Huber, Michael, Ph. D.
[Nikon SB-28 blitzsystem. English]
Nikon SB-28 AF speedlight / Michael Huber ; [translated by Phyllis M. Riefler-Bonham]. -- English language ed.
p. cm. -- (Magic lantern guides)
"A laterna magica book."
ISBN 1 883403-52-9 (pbk.)
1. Electronic flash photography--Handbooks, manuals, etc.
2. Nikon camera--Handbooks, manuals, etc. I. Title. II. Series.
TR606.H832313 1999
778.7'2 -- dc21 98-36469
CIP

Contents

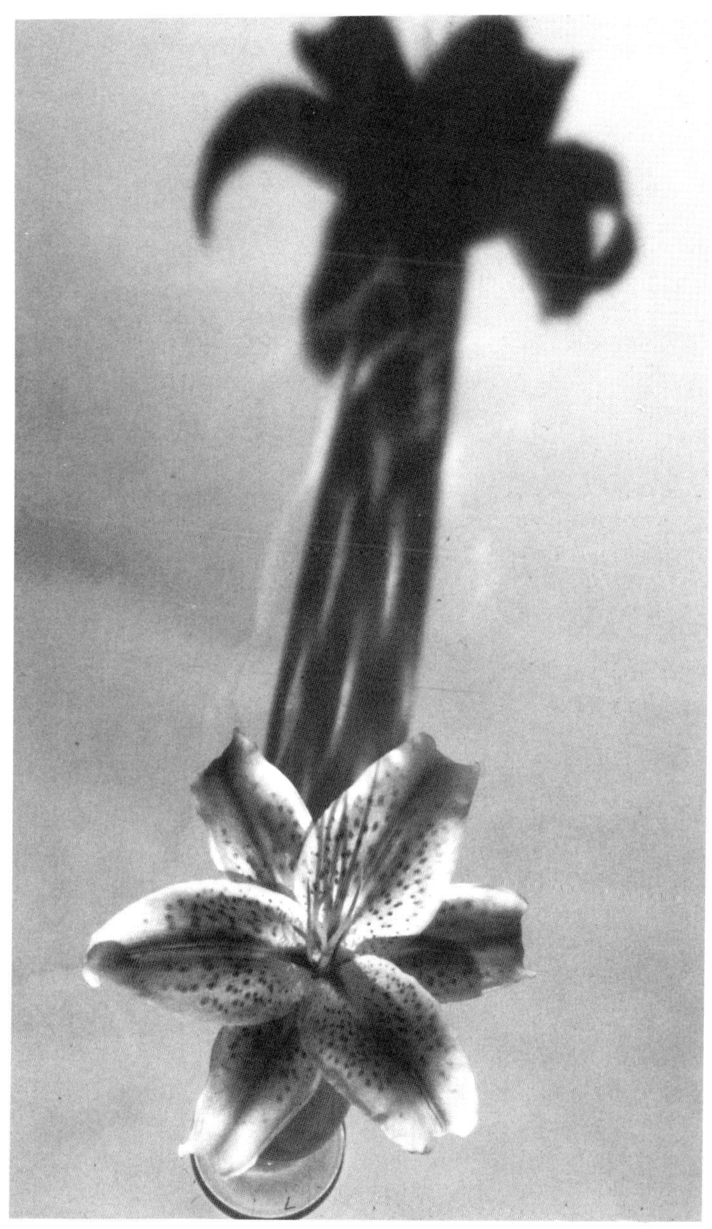

These photos demonstrate the importance of choosing the correct exposure method and the appropriate flash mode. They were photographed using the following techniques:

A) *Light measurement with hand-held exposure meter (1 sec. at f/5.6) without flash.*
B) *Matrix-balanced flash (1/125 sec. at f/4).*
C) *Conventional TTL (through-the-lens) flash (1/125 sec. at f/4).*
D) *Fully manual flash (1/125 sec. at f/11).*

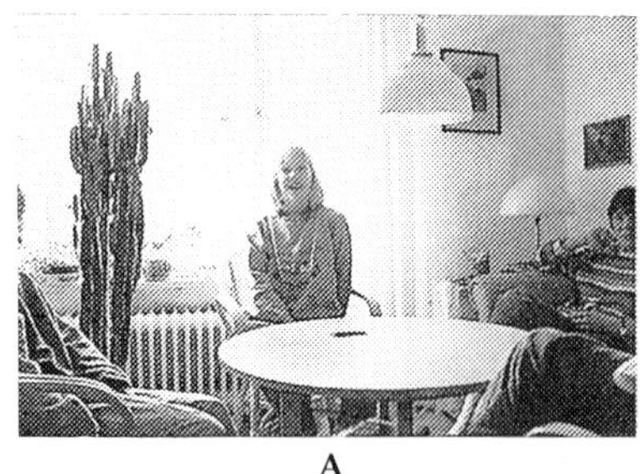

A

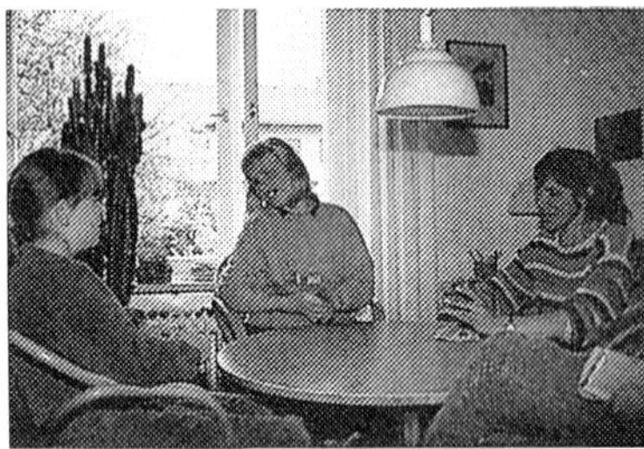

B

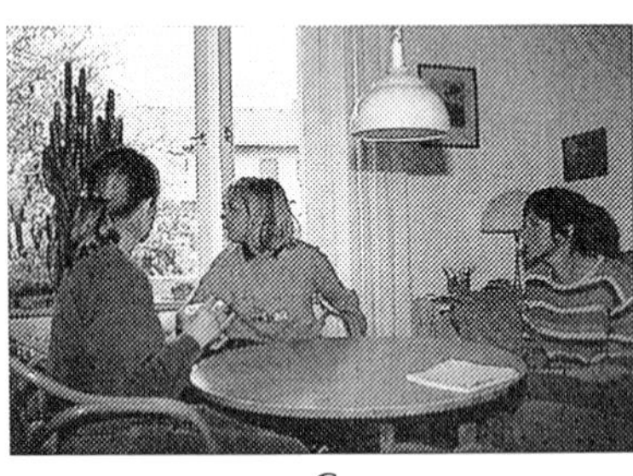

C

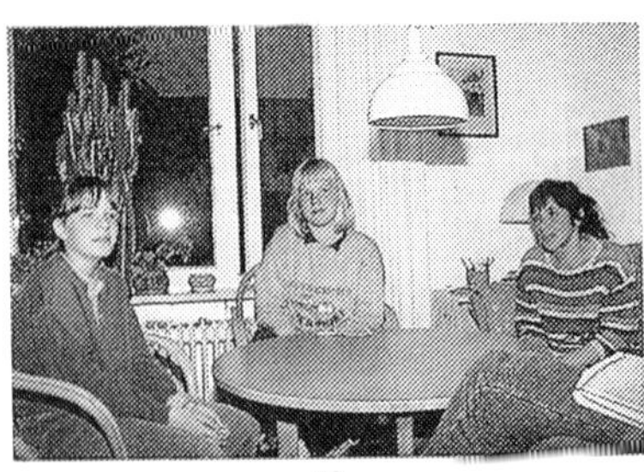

D

The need for the photographer to be well-versed in different flash techniques is clearly illustrated by the varying quality of these results. This manual is designed to help you get the best possible pictures using the many capabilities of the SB-28 AF Speedlight.

About This Manual

For Whom This Manual Was Written

While discussing this topic with amateur and professional photographers, it became obvious that most users take advantage of only a fraction of the capabilities of modern microprocessor-controlled camera systems. This is even more true when using flash. There are many combinations of TTL autoflash options with various exposure methods (from manual to several automatic program modes) and exposure-metering preferences (from spot to matrix metering). Since the introduction of microprocessor-controlled flash units and cameras in 1988, Nikon's multi-faceted flash technology has posed many problems for photographers. And, the expanded capabilities seen in combinations of the SB-28/F5 or SB-28/N90s (F90X), for example, have added to the confusion. Often, photographers will settle on one tried-and-true method, leaving unused all of the many remaining options offered by their camera/flash combination. This manual is intended for those who want to better understand the many innovative capabilities of the SB-28, even before purchasing this flash unit, in order to use its features to best advantage.

Differences Among SB-25, SB-26, and SB-28 Flash Systems

SB-28 = Ergonomically improved, compact version of the SB-26, offering enhanced flash capacity minus the slave/flash function

SB-26 – SB-25 plus torch-type red-eye reduction and slave/flash function

Apart from the differences mentioned above, many explanations regarding the SB-28 contained in this book will be applicable to both the SB-25 and SB-26 Flash Systems.

An Improved Instruction Guide

Optimum use of the SB-28 requires some background knowledge of flash technology. However, due to a reliance on today's sophisticated, automatic gadgetry, this knowledge is frequently riddled with gaps. Therefore, this manual includes a concise introduction to the fundamentals of flash technology and, as a result, goes far beyond a conventional instruction manual. In some areas, though, the book is intentionally brief, compared with operating manuals. It concentrates mainly on the use of the SB-28 with the N70/F70, N8008/F-801, N90/F90, F4, and F5 cameras. The buyer of an N5005/F-401X, N6006/F-601, or N50/F50 camera will hardly spend almost the same amount on a flash unit. Besides, the benefits gained from using the SB-28 will be relatively minor, compared with less expensive flash units for these cameras. The manual specifically covers the use of the SB-28 with the N90s/F90X or F5, as this combination represents the maximum capabilities of the SB-28 and highest degree of sophistication in automatic flash performance.

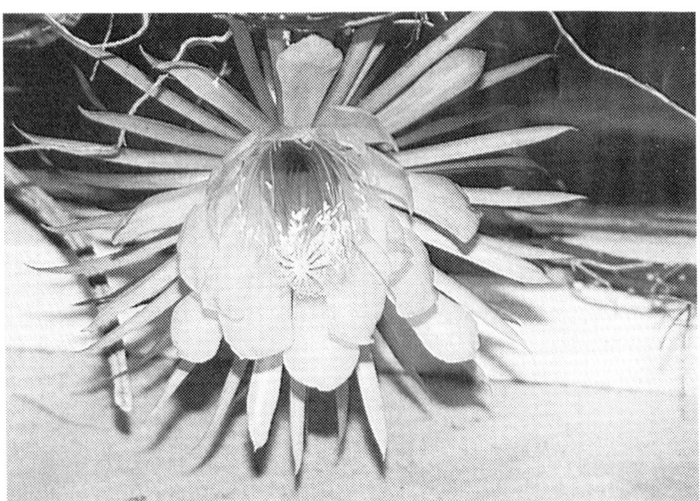

Focusing with the AF-Illuminator: *The photographer focused on this night flowering cereus in complete darkness, then made the exposure with flash.*

This manual also is intentionally brief when describing detailed procedures such as "First you push this button and then that button." Otherwise, all of the many minor differences among various camera models would have to be addressed, making the book cumbersome and confusing to the reader. The specific step-by-step procedures include instructions which apply to practically any SB-28 and camera combination for each flash method. You can find additional details in the SB-28 instruction manual which, of course, you should read completely. For additional information regarding specific Nikon cameras and accessories, refer to the camera manuals which are published by this company and are available for practically every current Nikon SLR camera.

Structure of This Manual

One shortcoming of many instruction manuals is the structure, which often emphasizes technical functions and different models instead of applications. Frequently, the user cannot see the "forest for the trees." This manual is organized so that you will first be introduced to the technology and the operating elements of the SB-28. Subsequent chapters will then deal with "where and how is it used?" Following this are chapters which cover how particular photographic situations and creative techniques can best be handled with the SB-28. Another chapter features the use of the flash in specific photographic applications. The last chapter offers a systematic introduction to the fundamentals of flash technology.

Regarding the Illustrations

Sample shots taken with the SB-25, SB-26, or SB-28 have been identified as such. Due to constraints of time and cost, I was not so much interested in the artistic and aesthetic aspects but, instead, attempted to re-create typical situations in which flash would be used. As a result, you may actually obtain similar photos under similar lighting conditions with similar subjects.

Thank You–

to Nikon Germany's Mrs. Schulz, Mr. Exner, Mr. Schmitt, and Mr. Matzky, who provided me with the necessary information to assure the success of this book.

Important Notes

Differences Among the SB-25, SB-26, and SB-28

Differences relating to using these flash units are not great. Therefore, many explanations regarding the SB-28 in this book are also

Shallow depth of field without background compensation with high-speed synchronization "FP": *Both pictures were taken at a distance of approximately 12 feet. The lens focal length was 180mm using an AF-D zoom Nikkor lens (80-200mm f/2.8 ED). In both cases, the flash exposure was taken at f/2.8 to create the relatively blurred background. The picture at the top was taken with program exposure, which selected a flash synchronization speed of 1/250 second (with 3D multi-sensor balanced fill-flash using the N90/F90 camera). The background is not only blurred but also relatively light at 1/250 second. The picture at the bottom was taken with high-speed sync "FP" with a manually selected shutter speed of 1/2000 second. We could debate which is the more aesthetically pleasing rendition; however, the comparison clearly illustrates that the FP mode produces a darker background.* ➢

Standard TTL-flash exposures with diffuser: *This snapshot was taken with TTL flash control, but without all the advanced features of modern automatic fill-flash units. The secret of this uniformly illuminated, not over-flashed exposure is a special diffuser in front of the flash reflector. This flash "ball" diffuses the flash with a brightness loss of only about 1-1/2 f/stops through a diffusion area of about 10 inches. This makes the light softer, with fewer hard-edged shadows cast by the subject. In addition, the light fall-off is visibly less drastic.* ➢➢

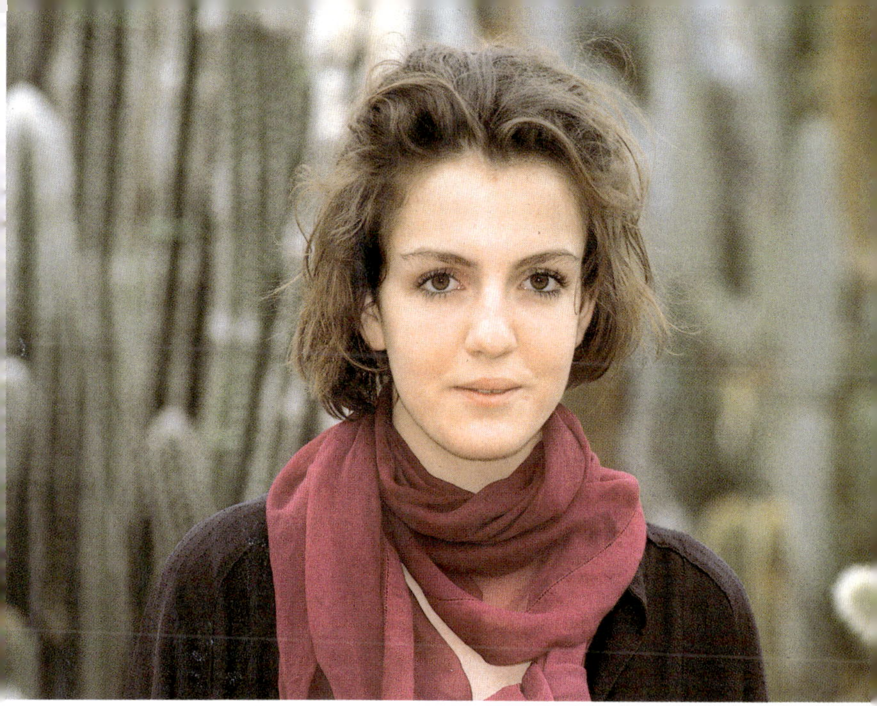

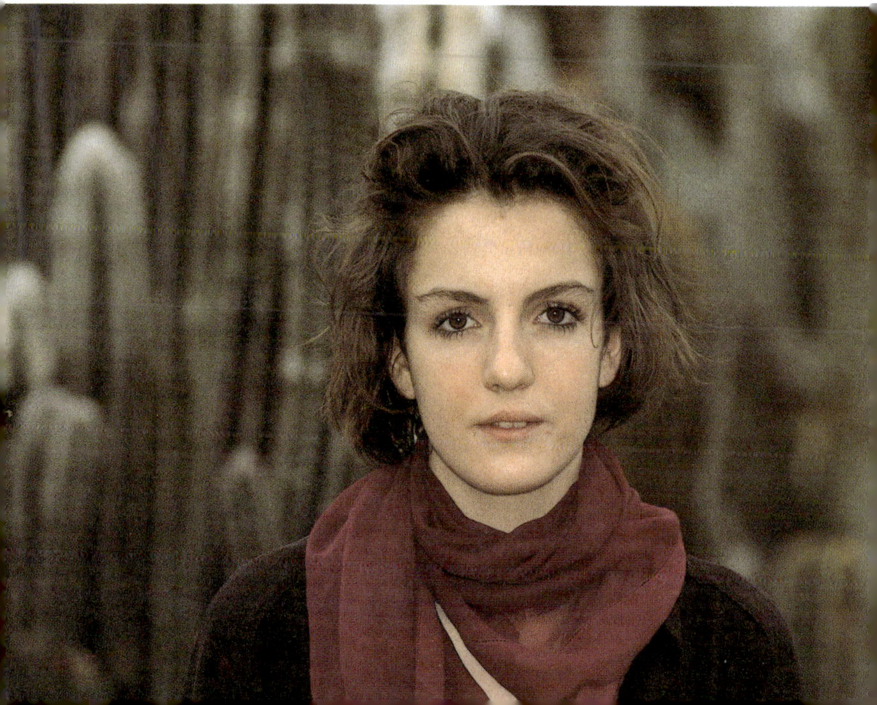

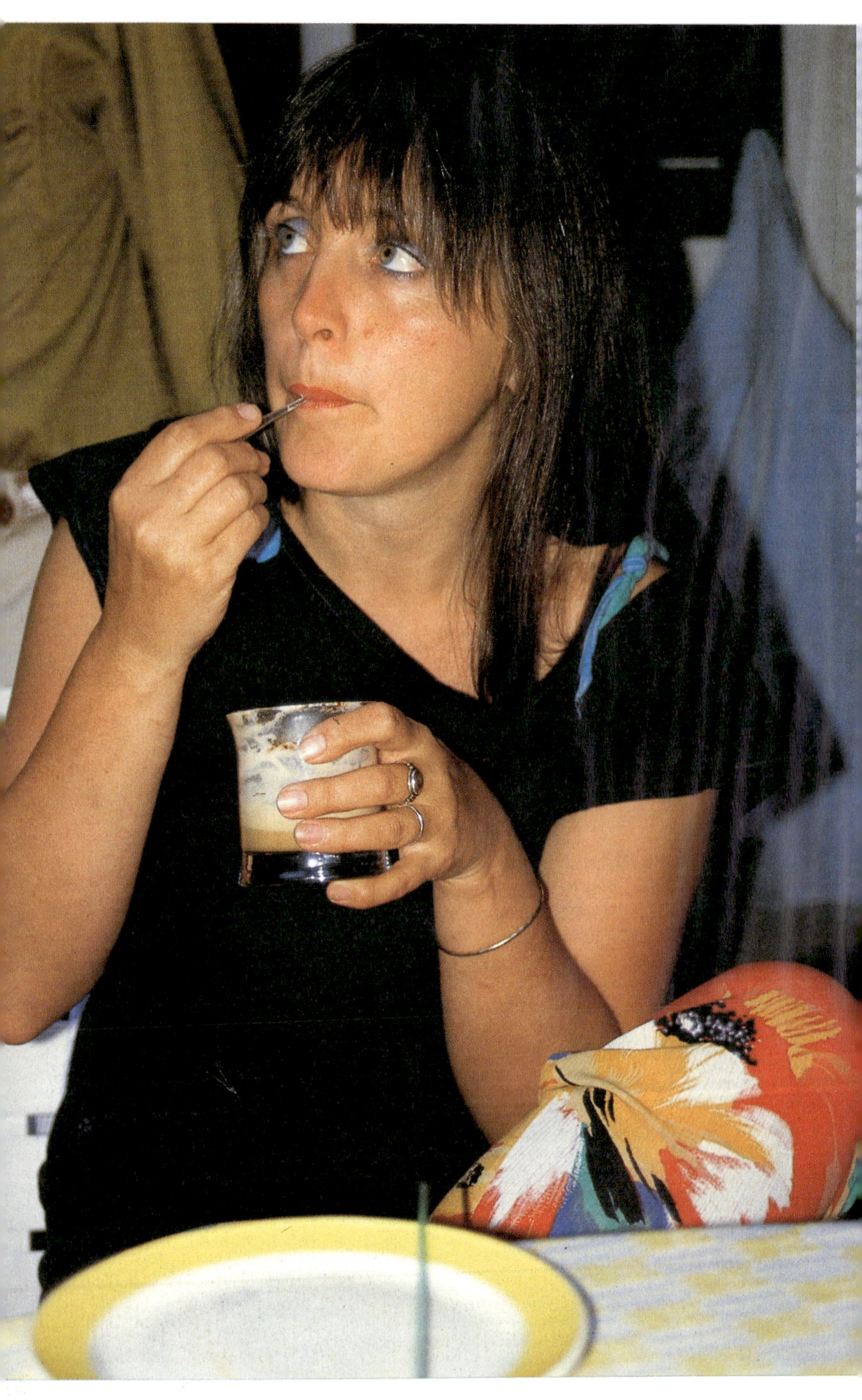

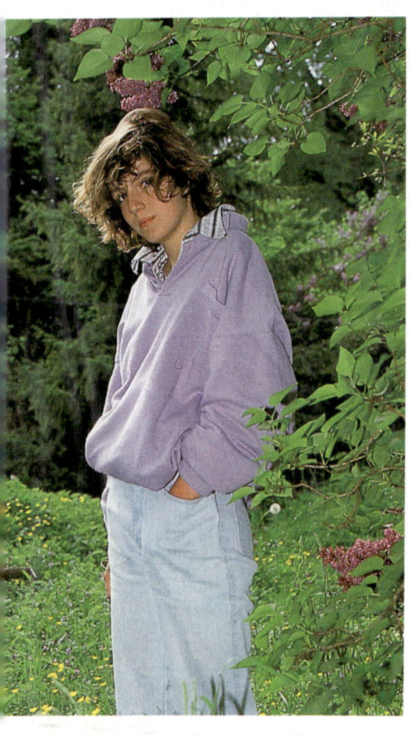

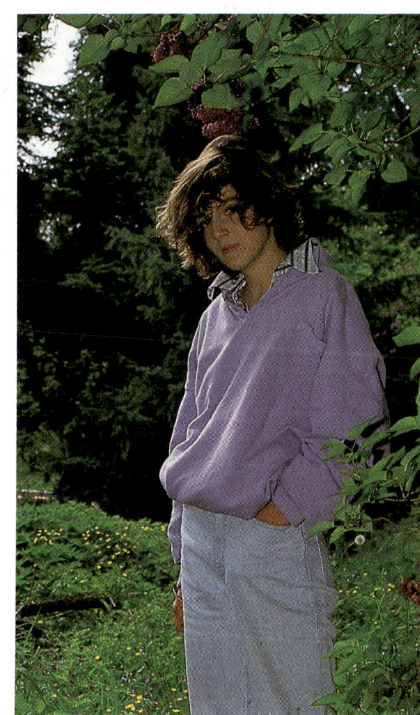

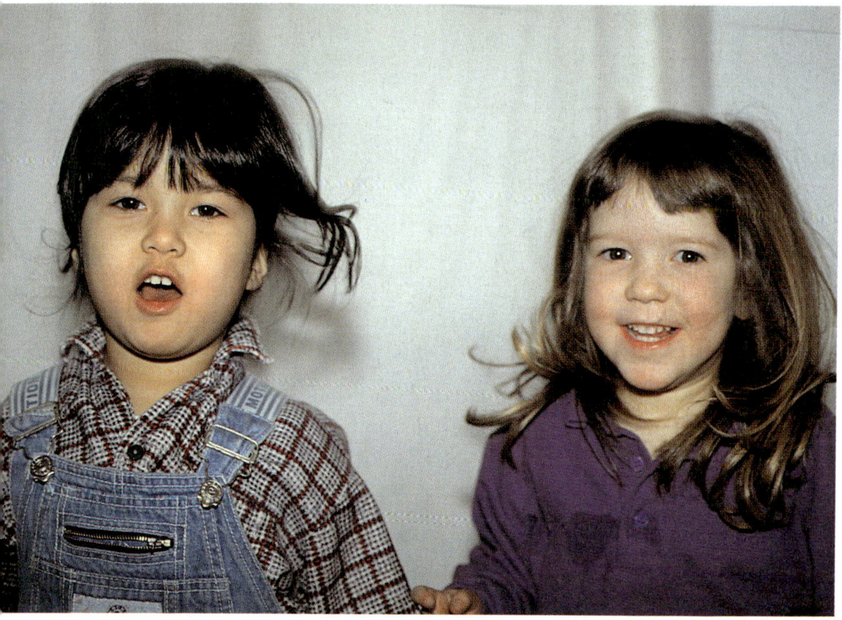

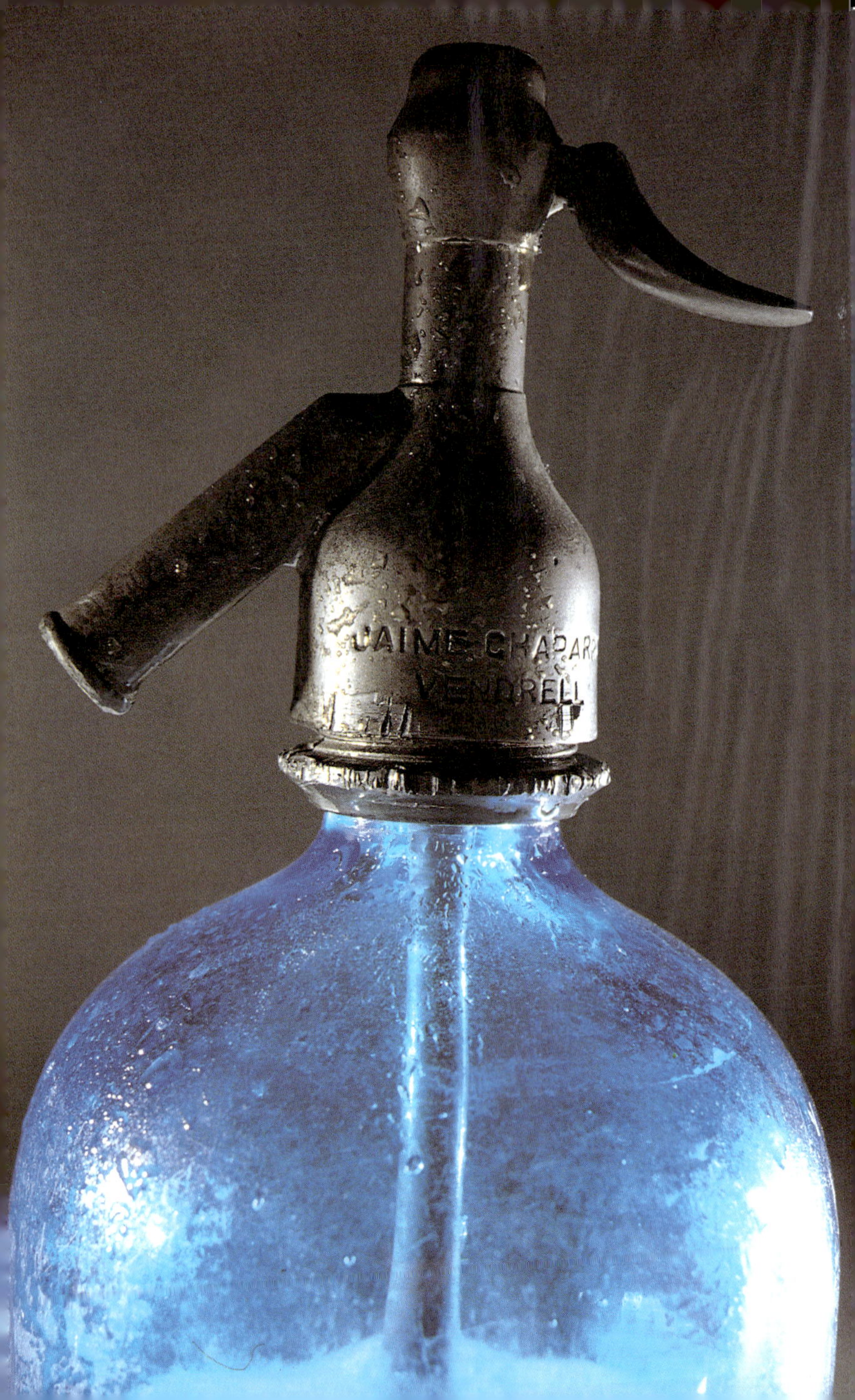
JAIME CHAPAR
VENDRELL

applicable to the SB-25 and SB-26. However, you should consult the original user manuals for the SB-25 and SB-26 regarding the use of the few different functions.

Camera Names and Models

From this point on, different versions of the same basic camera model are mentioned only if they are significant. For example, if "N8008/F-801" is mentioned, this would also include the N8008s/F-801s; if only "N90/F90" is mentioned, this would also apply to the N90s/F90X. The F90 is marketed as a package with the "S" and "D" model designations in some countries. The only difference is the addition of standard data backs: the MF-26 in the case of the F90S, and the MF-25 with the F90D. You can also purchase these data backs separately.

Verification

Due to time and expense constraints, it was not possible to verify in detail all the data and information provided by Nikon. Likewise, it was not possible to test all of the functions of the SB-28 with all cameras. I welcome your suggestions, should you find any inconsistencies.

<< ***Varying the background brightness:*** *Using manual aperture adjustment and standard TTL auto flash with a synchronization speed of 1/125 sec., one flash exposure was made at f/5.6 (top left) and one at f/11 (top right). Because the smaller aperture opening prevents the ambient light from registering, the background becomes darker. This example shows that with the use of standard TTL control and a not-too-light background, reasonably good results are possible without special automatic fill-flash.*

Red-eye reduction: *Thanks to the automatic 3D multi-sensor fill-flash used, this close-up portrait of two children was a success despite the extremely short shooting distance and light background. The preflash feature reduced the red-eye effect to the extent that it does not show in the photo.*

< ***Studio-type lighting with the use of TTL multiple flash:*** *This picture was taken with an AF-D Nikkor lens and 3D multi-sensor fill-flash, but with a manual adjustment of the aperture (f/16 at 1/125 sec.). The SB-28 was positioned on a diagonal axis from the right rear. An SB-23 was used diagonally from the left rear. The flash units were aligned by using home-made modeling lights (reflector lamps clamped under each flash). Thanks to the automatic flash features, the exposure was excellent. Due to targeted positioning and alignment of the flash units, it was possible to make the pewter shiny and the glass luminous.*

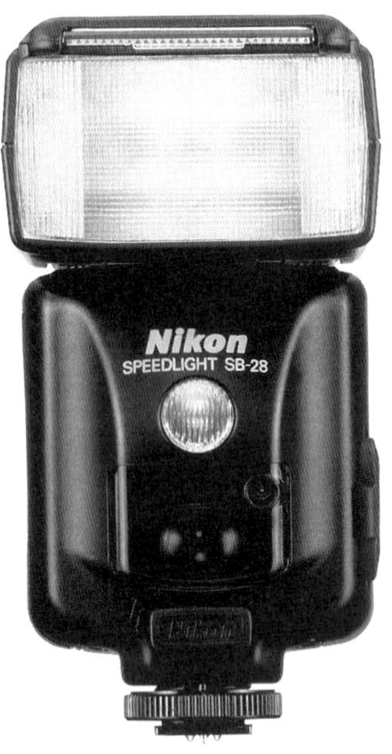
Nikon
SPEEDLIGHT SB-28

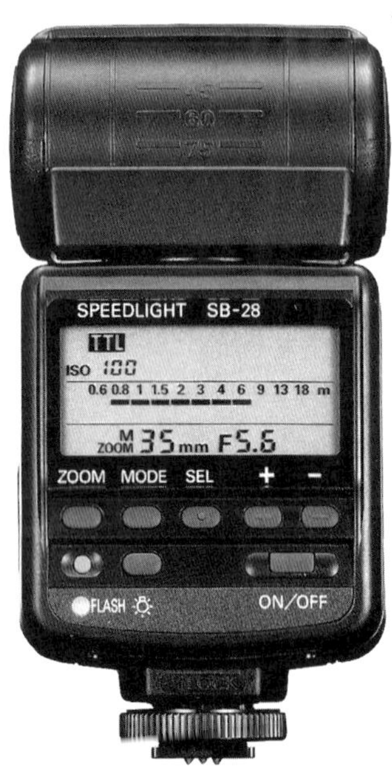
SPEEDLIGHT SB-28
TTL
ISO 100
0.6 0.8 1 1.5 2 3 4 6 9 13 18 m
M ZOOM 35mm F5.6
ZOOM MODE SEL + −
FLASH
ON/OFF

SB-28: The Best of Flash Technology

Compatibility

Nikon has long been recognized as a company that supports a system approach in its compatibility of equipment. I have found the SB-28 to be no exception to this philosophy, since it can be used with all previously manufactured Nikon SLR cameras. This is a great advantage for photographers, like me, who own more than one camera body. Of course, it's not likely that I would buy an SB-28 just for my FM2 camera. However, I would definitely buy one to use with my newer N90s/F90X camera. I could then use the SB-28, not only with its advantage of TTL 3D multi-sensor automatic flash, but also with my Nikon FA using the standard TTL autoflash mode. I could also use the flash unit with the FE or FM2 camera as a non-TTL automatic flash. Apart from this specific example, you can use the capabilities of the SB-28 to some extent with practically all Nikon SLRs. For example, the built-in AF illuminator assists AF focusing in low light or total darkness with all Nikon AF SLR cameras.

Enhanced User-Friendliness

As in the case of the SB-25 and the SB-26, settings for automatic flash mode, zoom-head position, and lens aperture are transferred fully automatically from modern cameras such as the N70/F70, N8008/F-801, F4, N90/F90, and F5 to the SB-28 flash unit. Therefore, little is left for the photographer to forget or adjust incorrectly.

The operating buttons of the SB-28 are rubber-coated for comfort and ease of operation. They are slightly recessed to prevent inadvertent actuation. The operating logic of the SB-28 could be better in distinguishing among function selection, function value setting, and locking against inadvertent adjustments. Still, you can adjust the SB-28 in less time, for example, than a digital watch. When compared with the SB-25 or the SB-26, the SB-28 definitely is more user-friendly from the viewpoint of ergonomics: By doing away with the sliding switches, a number of the confusing switch and push-button combinations were eliminated.

Display of Important Data

The SB-28 flash unit has an LCD which indicates selected distances or ranges, as well as apertures which can facilitate the use of manual and automatic flash functions. In addition, the operating status of the SB-28, ranging from the type of flash function to the zoom-head setting, is indicated. This display of information is invaluable.

High Guide Number and Seven Performance Settings

With an ISO 100-speed guide number of 118 at the 35mm zoom-head setting, or 138 at the 50mm setting, the SB-28 offers sufficient power for most situations occurring in action flash photography. Compared with the SB-26, this high guide number, plus a capacity of up to 100 flashes per set of alkaline batteries, shows how Nikon has successfully produced even more energy-efficient electronics. By using manual operation, the flash output can be reduced from 1/1 (full) through 1/2, 1/4, 1/8, 1/16, 1/32, to 1/64 power. As a result, you can usually work with a preferred f/stop or distance from the subject, even in the close-up range.

Variable Illumination

The motor-driven zoom head adjusts automatically for the focal length of the lens when using the SB-28 with the N70/F70, N8008/F-801, N90/F90, F4, and F5 cameras and 24mm to 85mm AF lenses. An additional built-in diffuser panel for use with an 18mm or 20mm lens increases the angle of illumination. This exceptional, wide-angle coverage places the SB-28 in a special position not only in the Nikon program but when compared to other flashes as well. The vertical-tilting flash head allows close-ups at -7° and evenly lit bounce flash exposures up to 90°. In addition, you can pivot the flash head on its horizontal axis by 270° to facilitate bounce flash exposures for vertical format shots, such as portraits.

Stroboscopic Function

The strobe (repeating flash) function can be used with practically all cameras. The calculation of the aperture setting and subject distance in correlation with the flash output has been solved particularly well. Strobe exposures, which, in the past, required considerable experience and many test shots, can now be taken effortlessly by almost anyone.

Synchronization With the Second Shutter Curtain

N90/F90, N70/F70, F5, N6006/F-601, and N6000/F-601m cameras allow optional synchronization with the second (or REAR) shutter curtain.

High-Speed Synchronization

In addition, the F5 and N90/F90 cameras offer high-speed synchronization "FP" (non-TTL) for shutter speeds up to 1/4000 second.

Red-Eye Reduction

The SB-28 offers red-eye reduction with the flash functions of the N70/F70 and N90/F90 cameras. A small lamp lights for about a second just before the exposure is made.

Preflash Monitoring for Greater Exposure Accuracy

With the automatic flash functions of the N70/F70, N90/F90, and F5 cameras, the SB-28 offers an invisible high-speed sequence of monitor preflashes to provide additional information regarding the reflectance of the subject.

Compatibility With All Power Sources

The SB-28 flash unit can be driven by a number of power sources. It is a high-performance unit which may be operated with alkaline batteries (in an emergency even with zinc carbon batteries), lithium batteries, or rechargeable NiCd (NiCad) battery packs, including the newer NiMH batteries.

External Battery Options Available

For those wishing to use an external power source, the SD-8a battery pack can be connected to the SB-28. This will decrease the flash recycling time to a minimum of 2 seconds and increase the battery capacity to a maximum of 350 flashes. Another option is offered by the SK-6A power bracket, which features a recycling time to a minimum of 2.5 seconds (NiCd batteries) and to a maximum of 300 flashes (lithium batteries).

SB-28: A Worthwhile Purchase

Those with an N70/F70, N90/F90, or F5 camera who want to experience the ultimate in modern flash technology should acquire an SB-28. For owners of N50/F50, N5005/F-401X, or N6006/F-601 cameras, the SB-28–compared with other high-performance (third-party) flash units–may seem a luxury, as the only additional features gained are with the use of strobe flash. Those who already use an N8008/F-801 or F4 camera with an SB-24, SB-25, or SB-26 will hardly benefit from buying an SB-28. However, those who now require a high-power "intelligent" flash unit will probably want to buy an N90s/F90X, F5, or future model in this new generation of cameras. From this perspective, the state-of-the-art SB-28 is a very worthwhile purchase.

Comparison of Some Nikon System Flash Units

Model No.	GN* (ft/m)	Focal Lengths	Flash Recycling Time (sec.)	Number of Flashes	AF-Illuminator	Automatic Fill-flash	Monitor Preflash	Preflash Red-eye Reduction	Slave Flash
SB-16B	105/32	28-85mm manual zoom head, 24mm diffuser panel	11	100	No	Yes	No	No	No
SB-23	66/20	35mm	2	400	Yes	Yes	No	No	No
SB-27	112/34	24 (35)-50 (70) automatic zoom head†	5	140	Yes	Yes	Yes‡	Yes§	No
SB-24	138/42	24-85mm automatic zoom head†	7	100	Yes	Yes	No	No	No
SB-25	138/42	24-85mm automatic zoom head, 20mm diffuser panel†	7	100	Yes	Yes	Yes‡	Yes§	No
SB-26	138/42	See above, plus 18mm diffuser panel	7	100	Yes	Yes	Yes‡	Yes§	Yes¶
SB-28	138/42	24-85mm automatic zoom head, 18mm diffuser panel†	6.5	150	Yes	Yes	Yes‡	Yes§	No

* The guide numbers in this overview table relate to ISO 100 and a focal length of 50mm.
† Automatic zoom head activated only with N8008s/F-801s, N70/F70, N90/F90, F4, F5, and AF lenses.
‡ Only with N70/F70, N90/F90, and F5 or, possibly, future camera models.
§ Only with N70/F70 and N90/F90 or, possibly, future camera models.
¶ With all cameras (N70/F70, N90/F90, F4, and F5 fully automatic correction of sync speed).

SB-28 Technology

This chapter gives a brief introduction to the operation of modern flash units, followed by an overview of SB-28 technical data. In addition to this information, you will find particularly important features, such as coverage, guide numbers, and zoom-head positions, listed in special tables.

Operating Microprocessor-Controlled Flash Units

If you look at the left side of the schematic, you will see the standard electrical circuit used for electronic flash units.

The flash discharge circuit: A flash capacitor is charged via a voltage transformer, which converts low-voltage direct current (DC) from batteries into alternating current (AC) voltage, raising it to approximately 300–600 volts via a rectifier. This capacitor stores the maximum energy available for each flash. As a result, the ignition coil first generates a short high-voltage firing pulse of approximately 1.5 to 3 kV. Then the stored flash energy of the capacitor is discharged at a voltage of approximately 500 volts. The noble gas atoms in the flash tube, which have been ionized and highly excited due to the discharge, release the electrical and thermal energy in the form of visible light. The duration of discharge is a function of the size and content of the flash tube, the flash voltage, and the resistor conditions in the electrical discharge circuit. At full output, the SB-28 has a flash duration (LT 1/1) of about 1/830 sec. At LT 1/64, the duration is about 1/8700 sec. Because the switching transistor can switch the current on and off, the flash duration (quantity of light released) can be controlled.

TTL flash metering in the camera: The light reflected off the film surface during flash exposure is measured in the camera. When the quantity of light measured (relative to the sensitivity of the film) corresponds to the correct exposure, a control pulse is generated to stop the flash discharge. While in some conventional

Flowchart of a Microprocessor-Controlled TTL Flash Unit

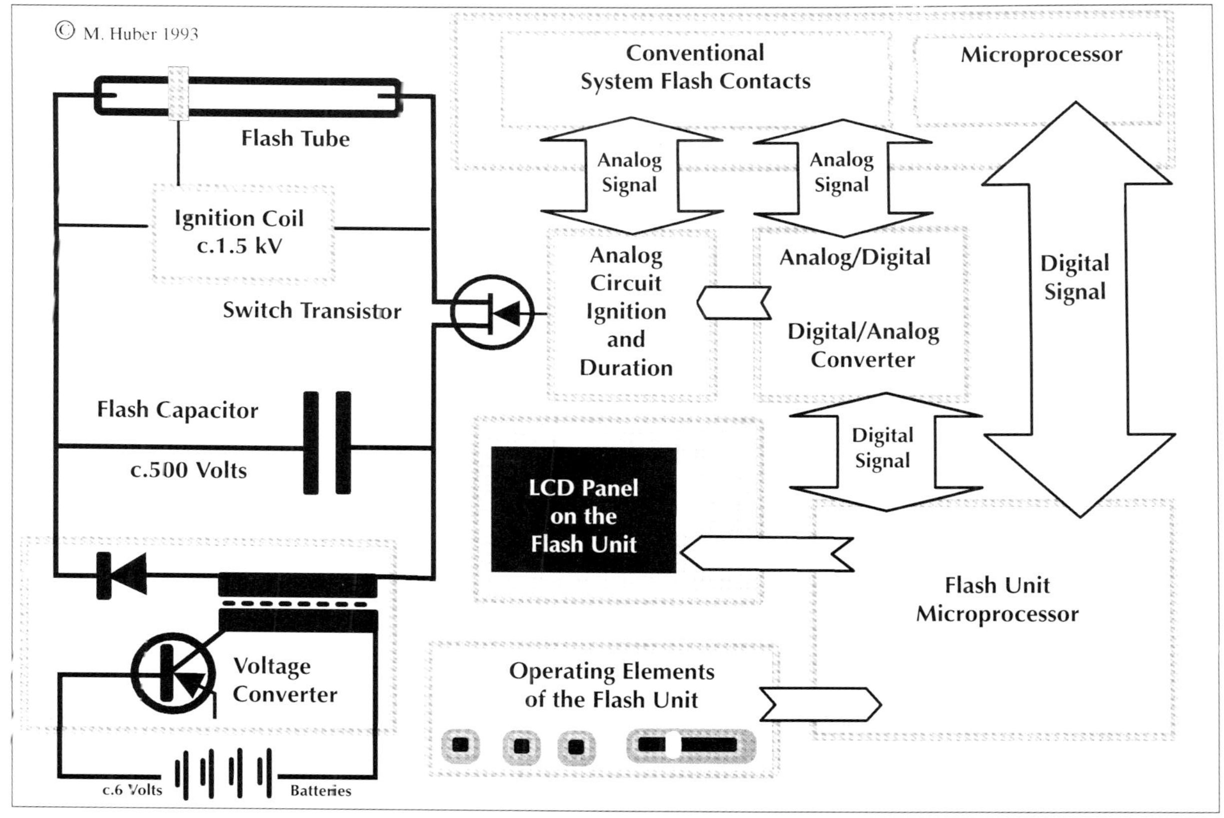

cameras this is still done via analog circuit technology, all values are largely computed digitally in the microprocessors of modern AF cameras. Only then, via systems contacts, will these cameras output signals converted into analog voltage pulses. As a result, even the most modern, fully electronic AF cameras are completely compatible with the older TTL system flash units. (You can find detailed information regarding the topic of TTL flash control in the chapter *The Basics of Flash Technology.*)

Analog feedback control for flash duration: The analog circuit controlling the flash discharge through the switching transistor receives an electrical pulse from the camera through the system's contacts. This fires and switches off the flash.

Variation of flash power: Besides flash duration, the amount of released flash energy can be controlled by varying the flash output. Principally, the maximum energy releasable by switching several flash capacitors on or off can be preset. In the SB-28, Nikon offers a variable resistor in the flash discharge circuit. Different from its predecessors, the SB-28 uses a combined control of flash energy via flash duration *and* flash output for manual flash exposures, as well as for automatic TTL exposures. This explains why the SB-28 features a relatively low variation of flash duration of only about 1:10 at flash durations between 1/1 (LZ) and 1/64 (LZ). In the final analysis, this means that the SB-28 offers more constant color temperature of flash illumination, compared with the SB-26, which features a variation of flash duration of up to about 1:23.

Analog data transfer between flash unit and camera: Cameras permitting TTL flash control provide information transfer in the form of control voltages from the flash unit to the camera. Depending on the camera model, an LED flash indicator (ready light) in the viewfinder is actuated to signal that the flash is ready to be fired and verify adequate flash exposure. Most camera models automatically select an appropriate shutter speed (flash sync speed) when the flash unit is activated. Even the automatic actuation of the flash unit from "Standby" takes place via analog signals. Although most modern cameras and flash units with built-in microcomputers are capable of digital transfer of information, Nikon still provides analog transfer to assure compatibility of modern cameras with older flash units or older cameras with modern flash units.

The flash unit's microprocessor: The microcomputer's main job is to establish the connection between the "user surface" (buttons and the LCD panel) and the internal control electronics. On the other hand, the microprocessor may also send digital information directly to the camera and receive digital information from the camera for evaluation. This does not necessarily require additional system contacts because, normally, digitized information can be added easily to the analog lines.

Digital data transfer between flash unit and camera: The duration of the flash is corrected on the SB-28 when used with N8008/F-801, N70/F70, N90/F90, F4, and F5 camera models. Digitized values are sent to the camera's computer which uses them in computing the TTL-controlled flash exposure. In the SB-28, flash synchronization is switched to the second shutter curtain on some cameras (N70/F70, N6006/F-601, N90/F90, and F5 models) and is transferred digitally to the flash unit.

Conversely, most modern Nikon cameras use digital transfer of the film sensitivity, aperture setting, and lens focal length to the SB-28 microcomputer. It uses these values to compute and indicate the distance range of the flash and/or automatic adjustment of the motorized zoom. This example proves that, thanks to bidirectional analog and digital signal transfer, the SB-28 is compatible with many diverse camera models.

SB-28 Specifications

Electronics: Microprocessor-controlled flash unit with bipolar insulating layer switching transistor (IGBT = Isolated Gate Bipolar Transistor).

Flash duration: 1/830 to 1/8700 sec. The relatively low variation assures almost constant color temperature.

Output	1/1	1/2	1/4	1/8	1/16	1/32	1/64
Flash Duration	1/830s	1/830s	1/1250s	1/1250s	1/4250s	1/6450s	1/8700s

Color temperature: Approximately 5600°K.

Guide number: The guide number is a function of the zoom-head position and the ISO film speed. (See *The Basics of Flash Technology.*) With ISO 100/21° at a temperature of 68°F (20°C), the values listed in the table apply.

Zoom Head: Focal Length, Coverage, and Guide Number

Focal Length	18mm	20mm	24mm	28mm	35mm	50mm	70mm	85mm
Coverage								
Horizontal	102°	98°	98°	70°	60°	46°	35°	31°
Vertical	90°	85°	60°	53°	45°	34°	26°	23°
Guide Number ft/m	60/18	66/20	98/30	105/32	118/36	138/42	157/48	164/50

Zoom head: Motor-driven, can be set between 24mm and 85mm. Coverage is set automatically when the flash is used with the N8008/F-801, N70/F70, N90/F90, F4, and F5 cameras and AF lens. An additional, manually activated wide-angle diffuser panel for coverage of an 18mm or 20mm lens is provided.

Auxiliary reflector/diffuser: Used with bounce flash exposures to attain highlights (such as, in the eyes).

Tilting flash head for close-up and bounce flash: With vertical stops from -7° to + 90°, horizontal from -90° to +180°. Locks automatically in standard position.

Power sources: Four AA alkaline or lithium batteries, or four AA NiCd or NiMH batteries. Additional external battery pack SD-8A or power bracket SK-6A.
Important: Only the European A-versions of external battery packs are compatible.

Flash recycling and number of flashes: With four fresh AA alkaline batteries at a temperature of approximately 68°F (20°C), approximately 150 full-output flashes may be triggered with a recycling time of 6.5 to 30 seconds.

Standby: The SB-28 automatically switches off approximately 80 seconds after firing a flash. With AF cameras, you can reactivate the SB-28 by lightly touching the camera release.

Flash modes: "TTL" (via the TTL sensor built into the camera); "A" (non-TTL with SB-28's integrated flash sensor); "M" (fully manual setting of the flash output); "Stroboscopic Flash" (repeating, low-power flash output).

Variable flash output (manual flash): Seven variable power increments from 1/1 (full) to 1/64 in 1/3-stop increments.

Synchronization: Select between the first ("NORMAL") and second ("REAR") shutter curtain sync. Use slow synchronization ("SLOW") with all appropriately equipped cameras–N6006/F-601, N70/F70, N90/F90, and F5 (strictly speaking, this is not a feature of the flash unit). Select FP for continuous flash discharge corresponding to synchronization at fast shutter speeds of 1/250 to 1/4000 second–N90/F90 and F5 only.

Flash control: The flash unit's ready light signals when the flash is sufficiently charged.

Low-light (insufficient flash) indicator with exact numerical values: Only with N70/F70, N90/F90, and F5 cameras up to -3 EV, in 1/3-stop increments. Other camera models will have only the ready pulse, no numerical readout.

Test-flash function: A flash test button is provided. Function "A" measures the reflected light via the sensor in the flash unit. It does not check TTL exposures.

AF-illuminator: Assists focusing in low light or even darkness with all Nikon AF SLR cameras.

Flash unit mounted in the shoe: This ensures that the flash is mounted with the flash contacts properly aligned for good connection with the camera. In some cameras, such as the N70/F70, N90/F90, F5, later F4, and later N6006/F-601, an additional pin engages with the shoe.

Red-eye reduction: Only with the N70/F70 and N90/F90 cameras. Like the SB-26, rather than the SB-25, the SB-28 features a small lamp.

Monitor preflash: For fine-tuning the automatic exposure; only with N70/F70, N90/F90, and F5 cameras. (See related section.)

Liquid crystal display (LCD): Displays all important data in a clear manner.

Display illumination: The LCD panel can be illuminated for about 16 seconds by pressing a button.

Rangefinder scale: Readily convertible between meters and feet.

Dimensions: Approximately 2.5 x 5 x 3.5 inches (65 x 127 x 91mm) W x H x D.

Weight: Approximately 11.8 ounces (335 g) without batteries.

Carrying case: Standard equipment.

Film Sensitivity Range

The film sensitivity of the SB-28 ranges from ISO 6 to ISO 8000 in manual mode. This range is restricted by the electronics of the camera that is used with the flash. Usable range is often ISO 25 to ISO 1000.

Distance and Aperture Ranges

The possible variation of aperture and distance range is a function of the film sensitivity with non-TTL automatic and TTL flash operation. The information given below reflects only the most relevant values.

Apertures and Shooting Distances in Non-TTL Automatic "A"

Film Sensitivity	**ISO 25**	**ISO 100**	**ISO 1000**
Smallest Aperture	8	16	45
Shooting Distance	2–3 ft	2–3 ft	2–5 ft
	0.6m – 1m	0.6m – 1m	0.6m – 1.5m
Largest Aperture	1.4	2	5.6
Distance Range	2-1/2–20 ft	3–30 ft	5–43 ft
	0.8m – 6m	1m – 9m	1.5m – 13m

Aperture and Shooting Distances with TTL Autoflash

Film Sensitivity	**ISO 25**	**ISO 100**	**ISO 1000**
Smallest Aperture	16	32	64
Shooting Distance	2 ft	2 ft	2–3 ft
	0.6m	0.6m	0.6m – 1m
Largest Aperture	1.4	1.4	4
Distance Range	2–1/2–20 ft	5–43 ft	6-1/2–59 ft
	0.8m – 6m	1.5m – 13m	2m – 18m

SB-28 Accessories

Cords and Adapters

TTL remote cord SC-17 for off-camera flash: One end of this 5-foot (1.5m) coiled cable has a flash connector which mounts on the flash shoe of all Nikon cameras equipped with a standard hot shoe. When mounted on the shoe, the SC-17 relays control signals, such as flash readiness status, TTL control, etc. The other

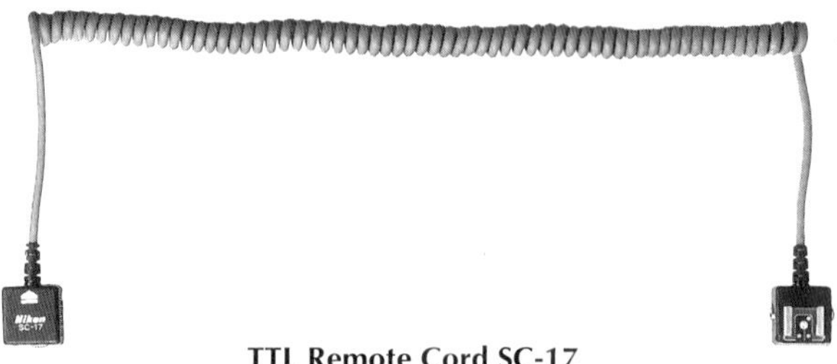

TTL Remote Cord SC-17

end of the cord has a standard hot shoe and two multiflash sockets for attaching any Nikon system flash or connecting additional flash units using SC-18 or SC-19 cords. With the N2000/F-301, N50/F50, N4004/F-401, N6006/F-601, N8008/F-801, F4, N70/F70, N90/F90, and F5 cameras, the SB-28 permits unrestricted TTL flash photography with all camera-specific options (even matrix-balanced fill-flash exposures). The SC-17 is indispensable when using the SB-28 with a Stroboframe® flash bracket.

TTL remote cord SC-24 for the F4 and F5 cameras: Permits TTL flash exposures when using the F4 and F5 with the waist-level finder DW-20 (DW-30 for F5), or the 6x high magnification finder DW-21 (DW-31 for F5) (neither of which have a flash mounting shoe). The SC-24 is a 5-foot (1.5m) coiled cable.

Slow synchronization and motion blurs: Both exposures were taken with the N90/F90 camera and a AF-D zoom Nikkor lens (28–70mm f/3.5–4.5) in programmed automatic mode. The picture on top was taken without flash; the slow shutter speed of about 2 seconds blurred the relatively dark motion streaks so that only the light center of the carnival ride is visible. The use of slow synchronization ("SLOW") and second shutter curtain ("REAR") sync in the bottom photo resulted in very pleasing, lifelike superimposition of the sharp flash image and the blurred motion effect. ➢

Motion effect with slow sync: Both pictures were taken with the N90/F90 camera and an AF-D Nikkor lens. Top: Programmed autoflash was used at f/4 and 1/60 sec. Bottom: Aperture priority mode was used with f/5.6 at 1/4 sec. (with slow synchronization). Due to the retention of detail along with the motion effect and the warmer color tones (light of the incandescent lamp is more noticeable), the picture at the bottom is much more successful in conveying the impression of a potter's wheel in action. ➢➢

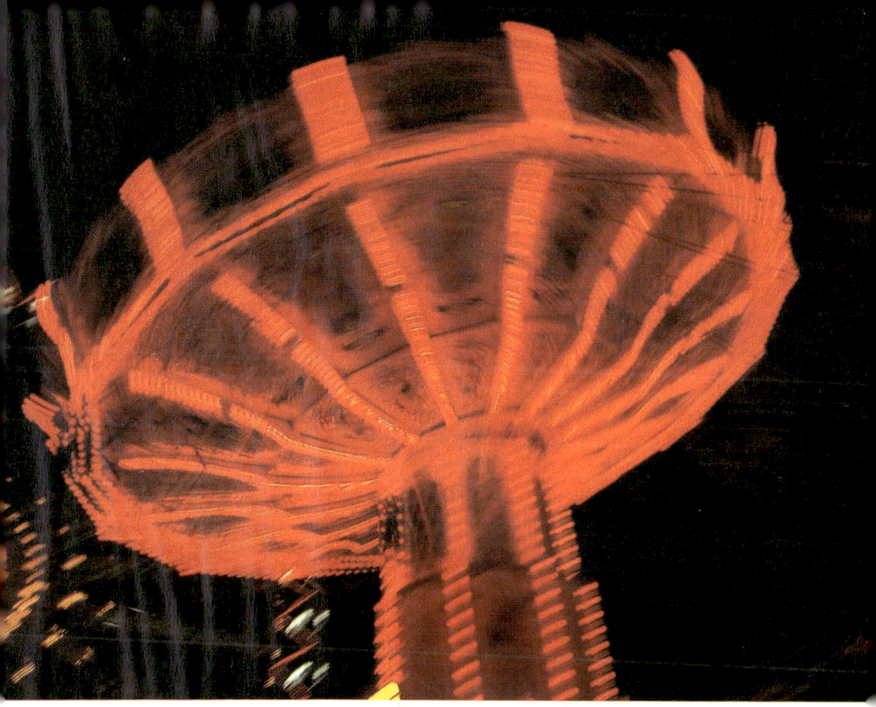

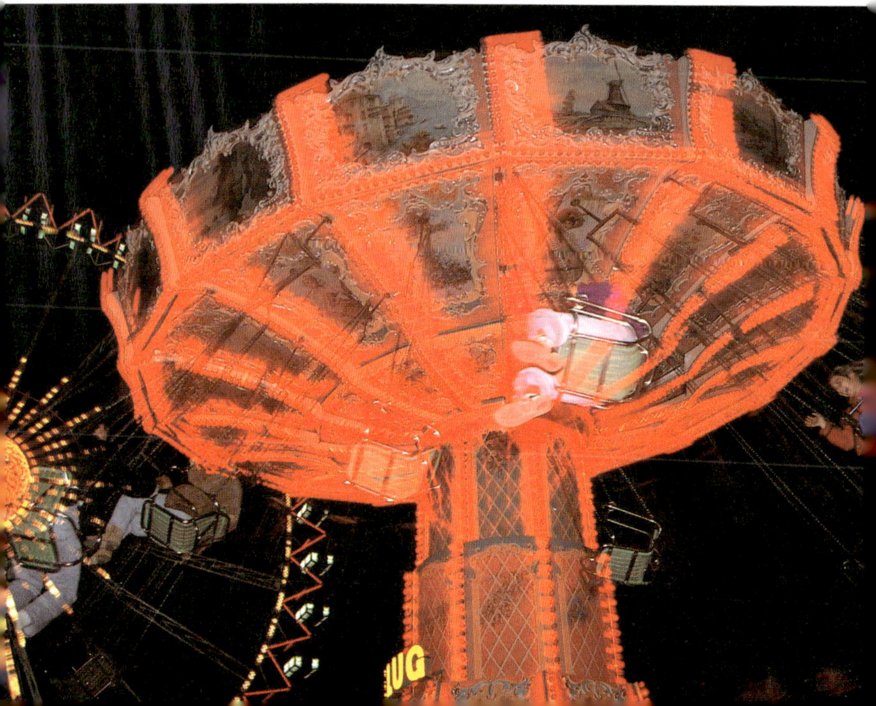

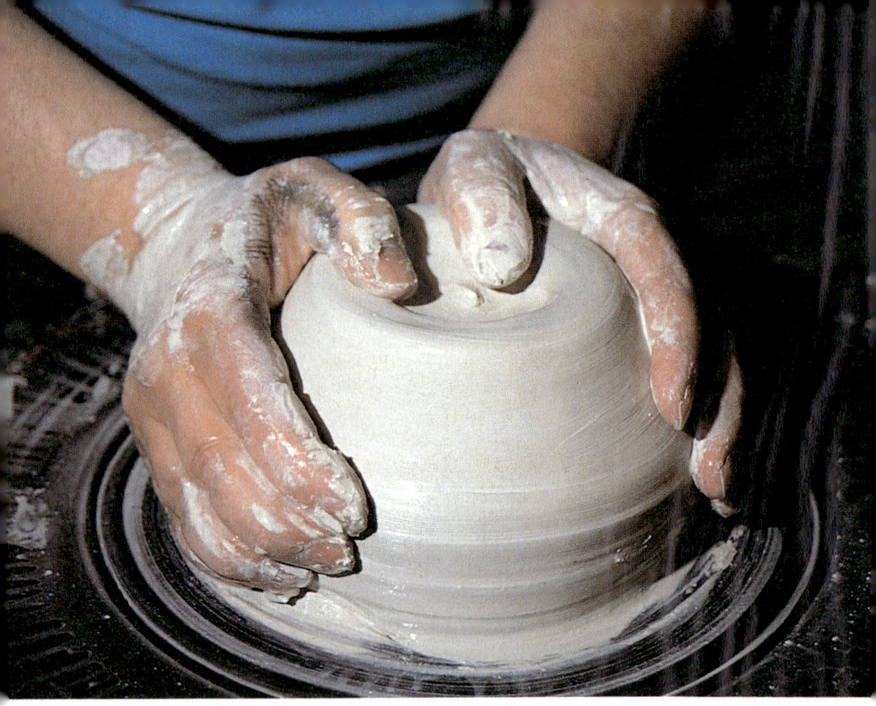

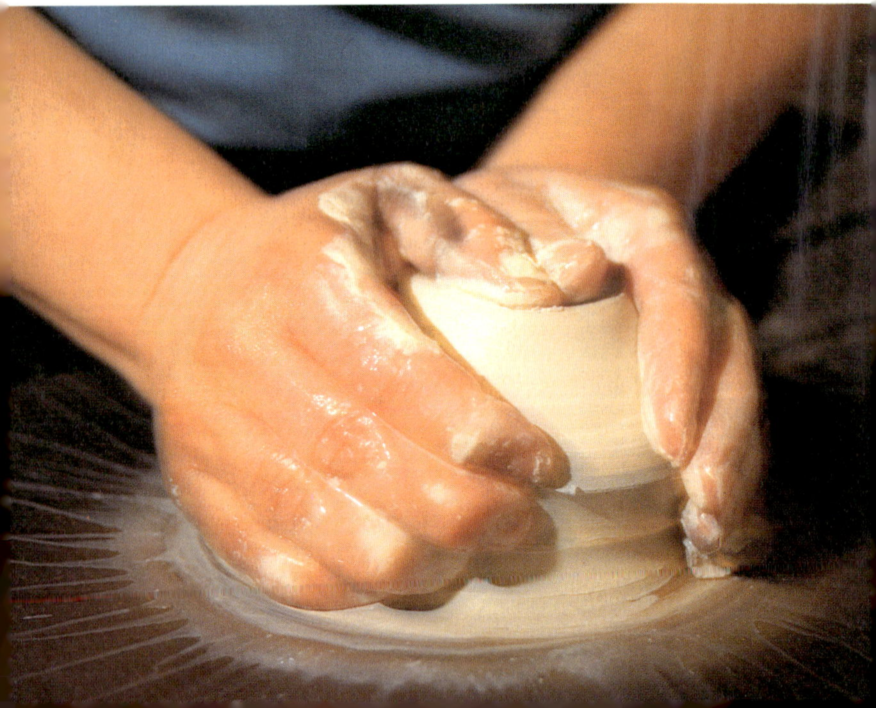

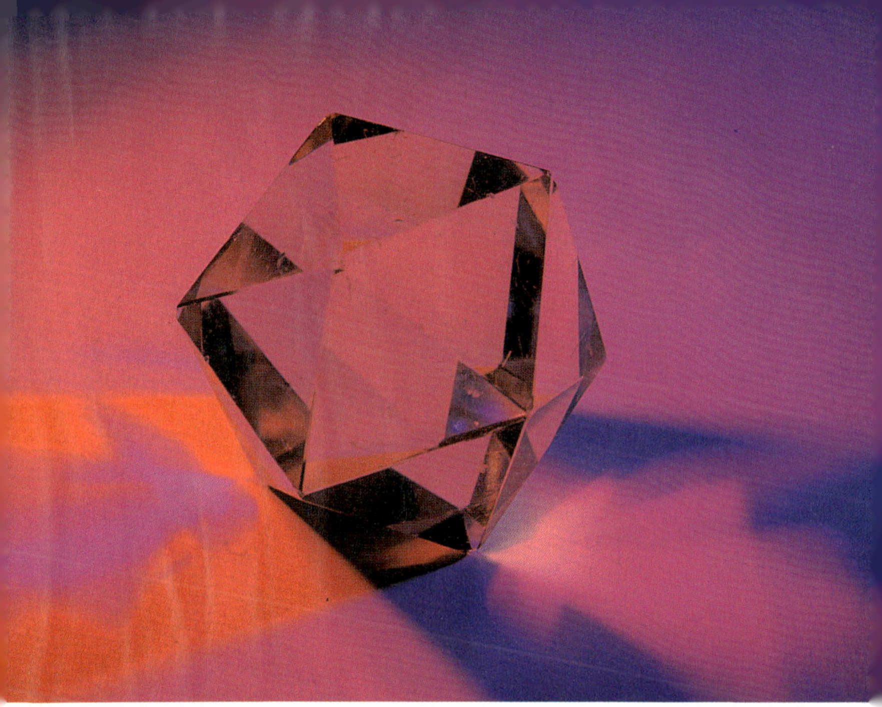

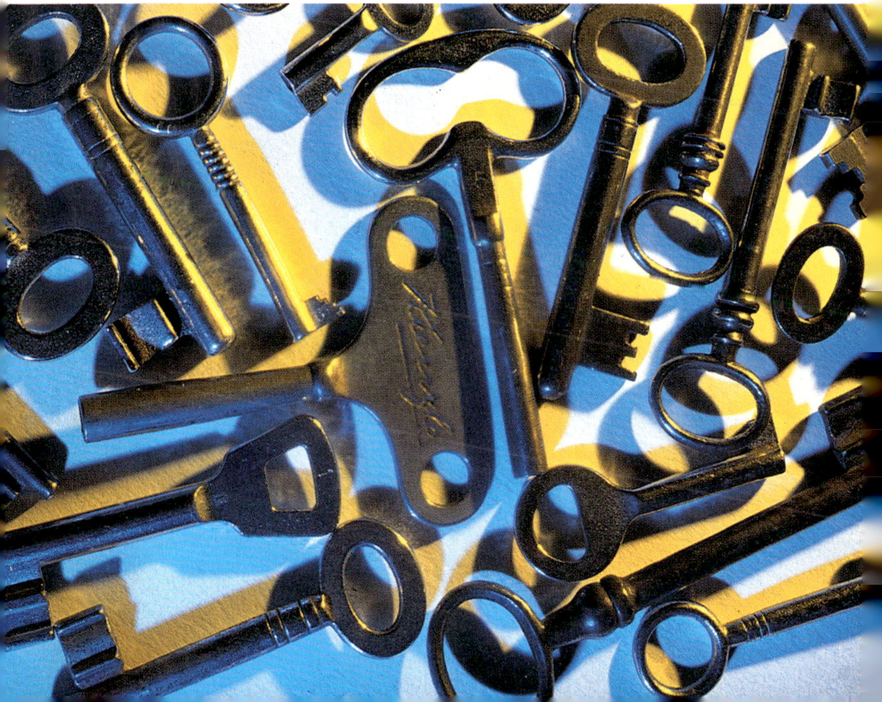

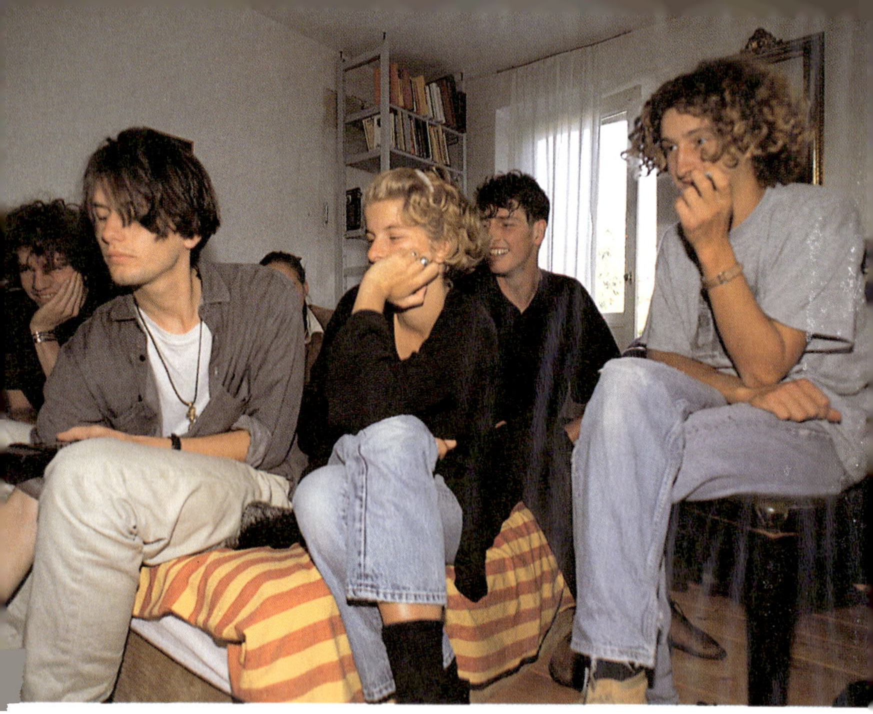

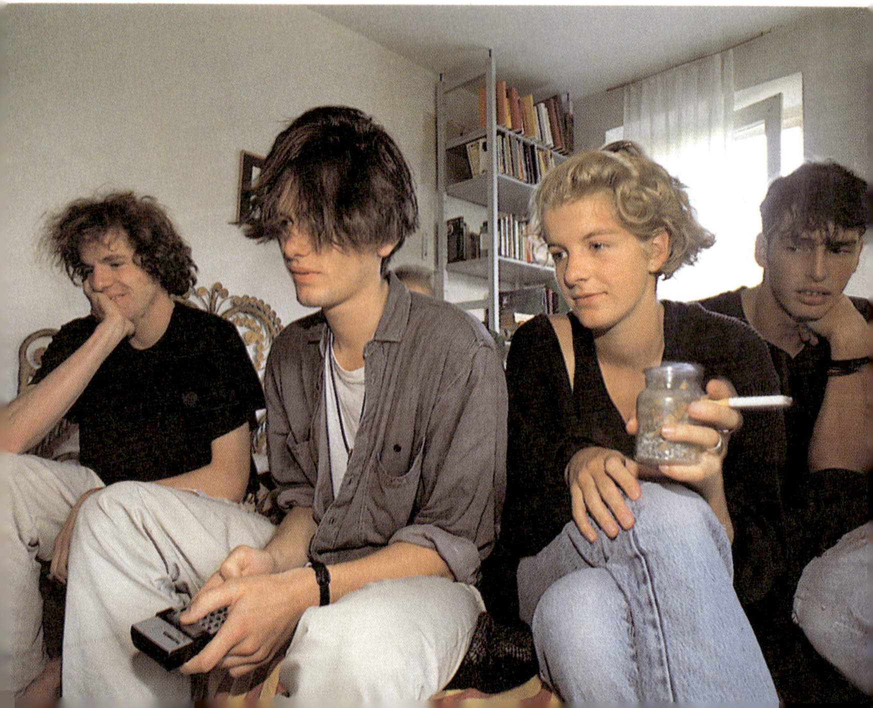

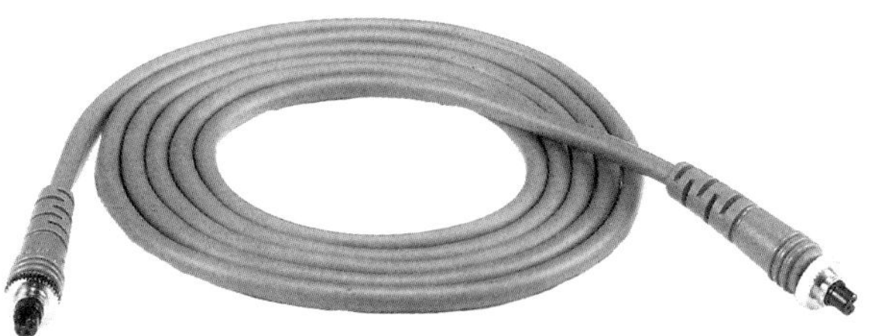

TTL Multiflash Sync Cord SC-18

Cords and Adapter for TTL Multiflash

The TTL multiflash sync cords SC-18 and SC-19 have terminals on each end for connection with Nikon multiflash system components (such as TTL remote cord SC-17, multiflash adapter AS-10, and Nikon system flash units including the SB-28). The SC-18 cord has a length of 5 feet (1.5m) and the SC-19, 10 feet (3m).

TTL multiflash adapter AS-10: For multiple flash. One flash unit may be mounted directly on the shoe of the AS-10 and additional flash units may be connected to any of the three multiflash sockets using an SC-18 or SC-19 cord.

Wireless Remote Flash Controller SU-4

This accessory allows true wireless TTL control with most Nikon Speedlight-series flash units, including the SB-28. See page 101.

Color effects in TTL multiflash mode: Two graphically interesting flash photos made with different color filters. An N90/F90 camera was used with an SB-25 and an SB-23 flash. **Note:** The TTL metering sensor is calibrated for "white" light and may require exposure compensation when using monochromatic light.

Balancing flash and ambient light: The foreground of this night shot was illuminated with flash. A slow shutter speed and large aperture were set on the camera to capture the ambient background light. A tripod was needed to prevent blur due to camera shake.

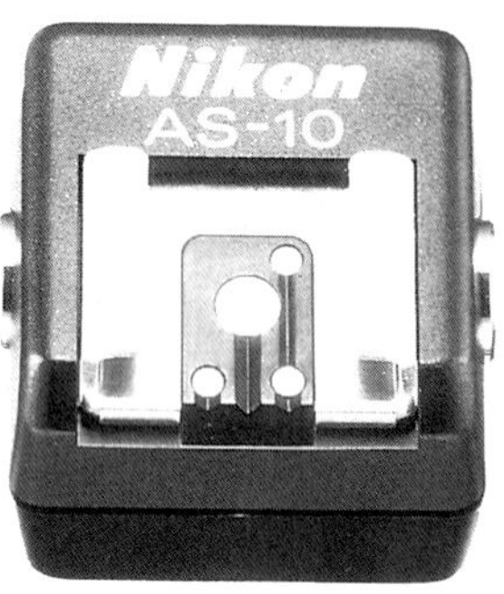

TTL Multiflash Adapter AS-10

Adapters for the Nikon F3

Flash adapter AS-4: For use when the SB-28 is mounted on the F3 camera's special flash shoe.

Important: The flash readiness status is transmitted; however, only automatic operation without TTL is possible.

Flash coupler AS-7: Allows film rewinding and opening of the F3 camera back while the SB-28 is mounted; only the flash readiness status will be transmitted and only automatic operation without TTL is possible.

Variable Stroboframe Flash Bracket

Nikon does not offer a comparable flash bracket. Nevertheless, I consider Stroboframe brackets useful for discussion at this point. These innovative flash brackets are manufactured and marketed by the Tiffen Company in the U.S.

Sturdy, sensible, modular design: The basic principle of this particular model is a sturdy, lightweight aircraft aluminum frame with ergonomically molded grips. The top bar of the bracket features a 1/4-20 machine screw for attaching dedicated cords. It also accepts standard flash mounts which are modular in design. The flash mount on the SC-17 remote cord can be securely attached with the standard 1/4-20 machine screw. A platform at the base of the bracket holds the camera securely.

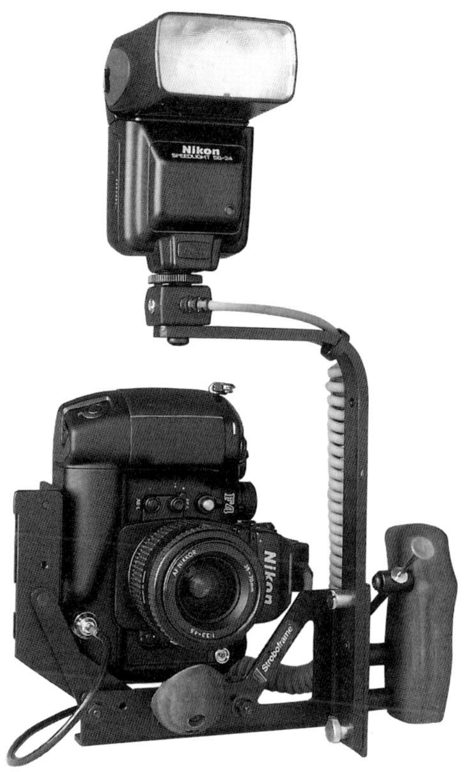

Stroboframe Flash Bracket

Advantages of using a Stroboframe bracket: Many professional photographers prefer to use off-camera flash because it offers better lighting control. Direct, on-camera flash is often harsh and unnatural with heavy, hard-edged shadows. When the flash is too close to the lens, red-eye can occur. This is a condition caused by the light from the flash reflecting from the inner eye, resulting in an unattractive, blood-shot appearance. One solution is to use bounce flash, but this technique has its own problems and limitations. Factors such as ceiling height, texture, or color can often cause unpredictable results.

A simple way to avoid undesirable results in flash photography is to use a well-designed bracket such as a Stroboframe bracket.

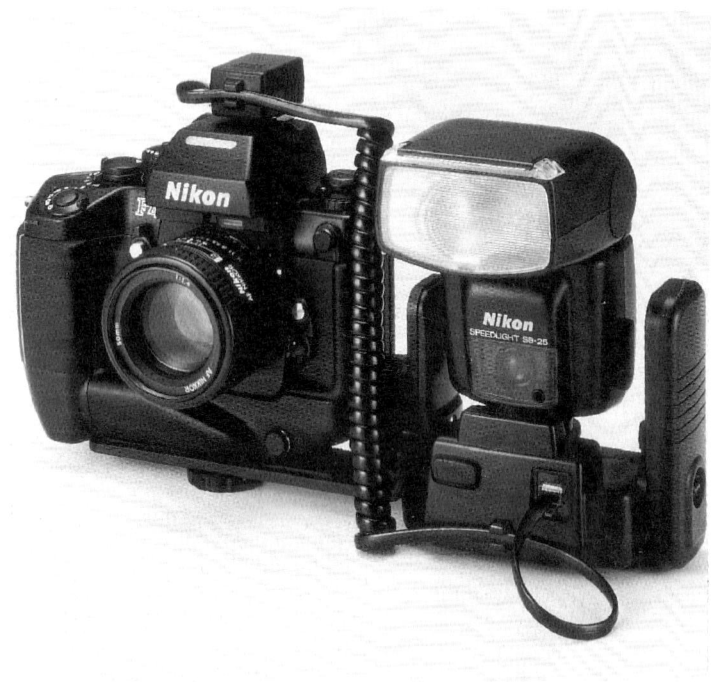

Power Bracket SK-6A

Using a bracket raises the flash to the correct height for a natural lighting effect. Shadows fall behind and below the subject and harsh edged "ghost" shadows are eliminated, even when the subject is close to the background.

One very interesting benefit of using a Stroboframe bracket is that you can rotate the camera platform easily between horizontal and vertical formats. The advantage is that the flash remains, at all times, centered above the camera in the same position for high, natural-looking lighting. Even though the SB-28, by itself, can be tilted for vertical and horizontal formats, the bracket maintains the ideal high-above-the-lens flash position. Also, time-consuming, repositioning of the flash head is not necessary.

Power Brackets SK-6 and SK-6A

The current international version of the SK-6 is suitable only for

SB-26, SB-25, SB-24, and SB-22 flash units. The SB-28 model distributed in Europe, however, requires the new European SK-6A power bracket version. (Due to stricter electrical safety regulations in the EU, the external power sockets of the SB-28 are different from those of its predecessors.)

A flash unit is usually mounted directly to the camera viewfinder. Often, this location is optically and mechanically not very convenient. Now the U-shaped SK-6 bracket protects the flash unit between an ergonomically shaped grip on the exterior bracket and a quickly releasable, yet sturdy, camera flange on the inside. This protects the flash unit against shocks, and the entire camera/flash combination can be handled safely. If you want to elevate the flash unit, you can detach the SK-6 from the camera quickly and hold it above your head.

The SK-6's integrated battery module offers fast recycling times (up to 2.5 seconds) and a higher number of flashes (up to 300).

With a Stroboframe bracket, the SB-28 also becomes a photojournalist's flash: It used to be that photojournalists would almost exclusively use side-mounted, handle-type flash units. One reason was that the bar-style bracket provided a secure support for the entire flash/camera combination, which is of great advantage when being jostled. Compared with this the SB-28 mounted directly on the shoe is rather unstable in one's hands. In addition, the connection between flash unit and camera is rather rigid so that impact with the flash unit might damage the camera's accessory shoe or the flash unit. A sturdy, well-engineered, Stroboframe flash bracket solves this problem. Along with the many lighting advantages listed above, SK-6/SK-6A power brackets or Stroboframe brackets are a distinct advantage for photojournalists as well as many other photographers.

Camera Compatibility

Most of the SB-28's automated features are fully realized only when it is used with the N70/F70, N90/F90, and F5 cameras. However, the flash unit is also compatible with other Nikon camera models including the classic F2 model. This means that the camera's electronics determine the capabilities of the SB-28.

Compatibility of the SB-28 With Nikon Cameras

	F5	N90 F90	N70 F70	F4	N8008 F-801	N6006 F-601	N50 F50	N5005 F-401X	N4004 F-401	N2020 F-501	N2000 F-301	FA	FE2	FG	F3	F2	FM2	FG20
FP high-speed synchronization	+	+																
Second ("Rear") shutter curtain synch	+	+	+															
Red-eye reduction		+	+															
Monitor preflash	+	+	+															
3D matrix TTL multi-sensor flash	+	+	+															
Matrix-balanced TTL fill-flash				+	+	+	+	+										
TTL fill-flash, spot/center-weighted	+	+	+	+	+	+	+	+										
Programmed TTL flash									+	+	+							
Standard TTL flash	+	+	+	+	+	+			+	+	+	+	+	+				
TTL flash in the macro range	+	+	+	+	+				+	+	+	+	+	+				
Manual flash exposure correction with TTL autoflash	+	+	+	+	+	(+)	(+)	(+)	(+)	(+)	(+)	(+)	(+)	(+)				
Non-TTL automatic flash mode ("A")	+	+	+	+	+	+	+	+	+	+	+	+	+	+	+	+	+	+
Fully manual flash mode	+	+	+	+	+	+	+	+	+	+	+	+	+	+	+	+	+	+
Manual flash mode with reduced flash output	+	+	+	+	+	+	+	+	+	+	+	+	+	+	+	+	+	+
Stroboscopic flash mode	+	+	+	+	+	+	+	+	+	+	+	+	+	+	+	+	+	+
Standby	+	+	+	+	+	+	+	+	+	+	+	+	+	+			+	+
Test flash (with flash unit sensor)	+	+	+	+	+	+	+	+	+	+	+	+	+	+	+	+	+	+
Non-TTL multiflash	+	+	+	+	+	+	+	+	+	+	+	+	+	+	+	+	+	+
TTL multiflash	+	+	+	+	+	+	+	+	+	+	+	+	+	+				

Using the SB-28

The following chapter is meant to provide you with a brief, but thorough, explanation of the operation of the SB-28. Now that you have invested in this state-of-the-art flash unit, it would be a pity if you used only a fraction of the many options offered by your camera/flash combination. Therefore, it is highly beneficial to totally familiarize yourself with its operation.

Liquid Crystal Display (LCD)

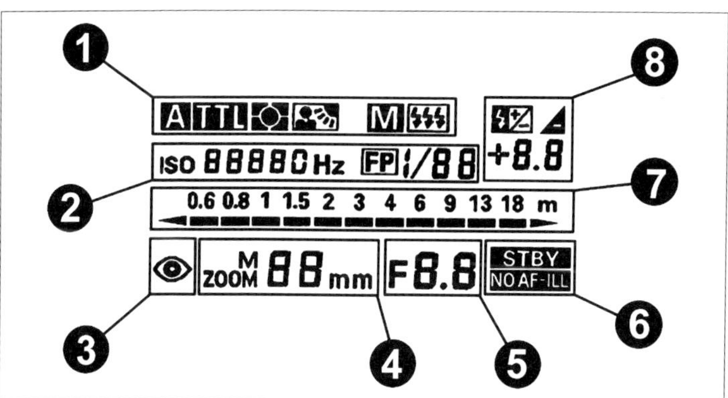

1) Flash mode indicator: "A" = non-TTL flash mode; TTL = TTL flash mode; matrix symbol = TTL multi-sensor flash mode; fill-flash symbol = TTL fill flash (non-AF lenses); "M" = manual flash control; multiflash symbol – stroboscopic flash.
2) Film-speed indicators: number and flash frequency with stroboscopic flashes; high-seed sync "FP"; power level (in manual flash mode).
3) Indicator symbol for red-eye reduction.
4) Indicators for motorized zoom head: focal length and function status; "M" for manual setting; blinking "M" when locked in a specific focal length.
5) Indication of actual aperture.
6) Indicators for standby mode or deactivated AF-illuminator status.
7) Indicator bar for flash distance range.
8) Indicators for flash exposure compensation or numerical indication of underexposure value.

Operating Controls and Features

1) Main "ON/OFF" power switch.
2) Plus and minus buttons for scrolling through numerical setting values for the currently selected function (e.g., ISO value for film sensitivity, aperture values, distance, and exposure compensation).
3) Liquid crystal display (LCD).
4) Scale for vertical zoom-head tilting.
5) "SEL" selector button for the desired function (e.g., film sensitivity and f/stop).
6) "MODE" button for basic mode selection (Manual, Strobe, non-TTL automatic, TTL).
7) "ZOOM" button for manual setting of the flash zoom head (e.g., for switching between 18mm and 20mm with pull-out diffuser panel).
8) "FLASH" test-flash button ("Manual release") with separate flash control indicator lamp.
9) LCD illuminator button.
10) Non-TTL automatic flash sensor.
11) TTL multiflash socket and conventional ISO flash socket (under protective cover).
12) Main diffuser.
13) Diffuser panel can be pulled out and down for 18mm or 20mm lens focal lengths.
14) Auxiliary panel. Can be pulled out for highlights with bounce flash.

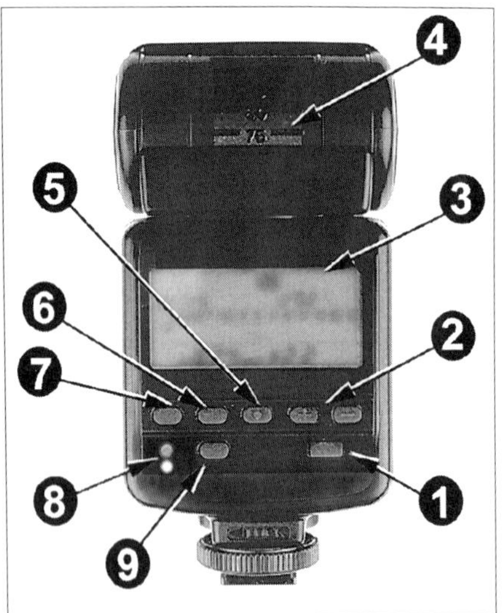

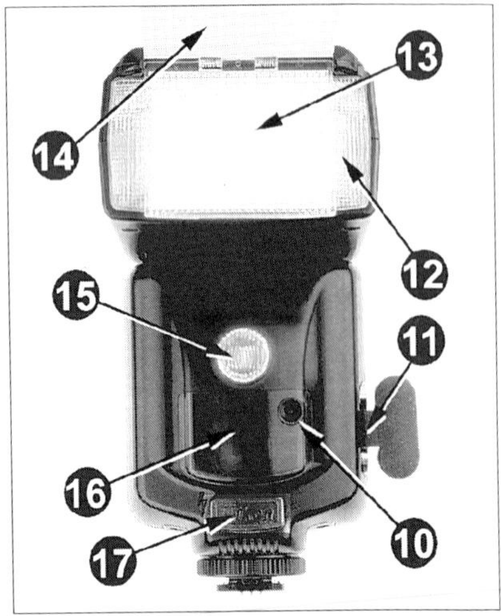

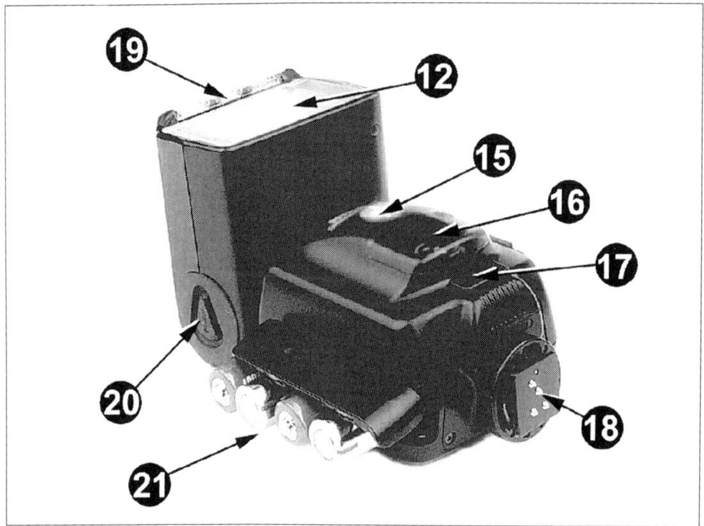

15) Red-eye reduction lamp.
16) AF-illuminator (auxiliary illuminator for automatic focus in the dark).
17) External power supply port (with protective cover).
18) Mounting foot with flash contacts. (Central, conventional ISO contact, plus three systems contacts and an additional locking pin for cameras with appropriate flash shoe).
19) Auxiliary diffuser and diffuser panel shown pushed in.
20) Lock release for vertical tilt and horizontal rotation of flash head.
21) Battery compartment.

Step-by-Step Operation

Following is a brief introduction to the steps in basic operation of the SB-28, with references to common problem areas, sources of misunderstandings, etc.

Loading the Batteries

It's obvious, and also important, that you insert batteries in the battery compartment with the contacts properly aligned.

Setting the Film Speed

The film sensitivity is transferred automatically to the SB-28 only when N70/F70, N90/F90, F4, F5, and N8008/F-801 cameras are used. All other cameras require the setting of the ISO film speed on the SB-28 itself:

- Switch the flash unit OFF and then ON again: The numerical indication for ISO values is blinking.
- Set the ISO value by means of the plus/minus buttons.
- Press the "SEL" button for activation.

Mounting the Unit on the Camera

Be sure that the flash foot is seated properly in the camera's flash shoe, then tighten the locking screw. (See "Flash Control Features.")

Selecting the Flash Operating Mode

Use the "MODE" button to select the main operating mode among TTL autoflash–"TTL," stroboscopic–multiflash symbol, manual flash–"M," and non-TTL automatic flash–"A." The selected flash mode is indicated on the LCD panel.

Selecting Slow and Second Shutter Curtain Synchronization

The SB-28 does not offer these features on the flash unit itself. Desired values must be set on suitable cameras such as the N6006/F-601, N70/F70, N90/F90, and F5.

Adjusting the Zoom Head

When AF Nikkor lenses are used with N8008/F-801, N70/F70, F4, F5, and N90/F90 cameras, the zoom head is adjusted automatically. With non-AF Nikkor lenses or with all other cameras, the zoom head must be adjusted manually by pressing the zoom button. With all cameras, the 18mm/20mm diffuser panel must be pulled out and down manually and the head manually zoomed from 18 to 20mm.

Flash Head Position

The normal, locked position is facing forward. To adjust the flash-head position, release the lateral lock lever. If the -7° tilt feature is in use, the range indicator blinks to remind you that the flash head is not in the normal position. In any other non-normal position, such as bounce, the distance scale (bar) is blank since the flash cannot gauge what the potential range would be.

Determining the Distance With Preset Aperture

When using the flash modes "M" and "TTL" with the N8008/F-801, N70/F70, F4, F5, and N90/F90 cameras and AF Nikkor lenses, the selected aperture value is automatically transferred to the SB-28. For correct exposure-range information with non-AF Nikkor lenses or with all other cameras, the f/stop must first be set on the lens and then manually on the SB-28.

- If necessary, press the "SEL" button.
- Set f/stop by pressing the plus/minus buttons.
- The bar-shaped distance scale on the LCD indicates the permissible distance setting (manual flash) or distance range (TTL flash).

Determining the Aperture for a Predetermined Distance

N8008/F-801, N70/F70, F4, F5, and N90/F90 cameras, used with AF Nikkor lenses, require that the aperture be adjusted on the camera lens until the LCD on the SB-28 indicates the desired distance or distance range. With the use of non-AF Nikkor lenses or with all other cameras, you must adjust the aperture on the SB-28 until (see above) the desired distance setting is indicated on the LCD display. You then set this aperture value on the lens.

Changing the Output Level

In "M" mode, the plus/minus button may be pressed for a continuous selection of flash output from 1/1 to 1/64 in increments of 1/3 f/stops.

Flash Exposure Compensation

If your camera allows, you may make flash exposure adjustments in TTL mode on the SB-28. Use the plus/minus keys to select the desired correction value in 1/3-stop increments from plus one to minus three.

Power Options

Battery Choices

Principally, all 1.5-volt AA batteries may be used in the SB-28, whether they are alkaline, zinc carbon, or lithium batteries. As an alternative, you also can use rechargeable NiMH and NiCd batteries of this size.

Alkaline batteries: AA alkaline batteries are available in almost any camera store, "mom and pop" store, or supermarket. These certainly continue to be the most popular power source.

Tip: Some types can be recharged up to 100 times with special battery chargers.

Zinc carbon batteries: These are less expensive and not environmentally hazardous. However, they offer lower capacity and are not stable when stored (they tend to discharge internally and leak). In addition, their cold-temperature response is poorer than that of alkaline batteries. Use them only in emergencies.

Lithium batteries: 3- and 6-volt lithium batteries have been sold for several years. Now they also are offered in 1.5-volt size AA. Theoretically, they would be the ideal emergency back-up for camera and flash units because of their practically unlimited shelf life (only approximately 10% self-discharge in 10 years).

It remains to be seen whether these new 1.5-volt, AA lithium batteries will have the high power-carrying capacity required by flash units. At this point, Nikon is currently recommending against the use of the 1.5-volt AA lithium battery for use in its products. If you are interested in using these batteries in the SB-28, I recommend that you keep updated on their acceptance by Nikon for use in flash units.

Tip: Lithium batteries are ideal as back-ups.

NiCd batteries: Because nickel-cadmium batteries exhibit higher current delivery than other types of batteries, they produce a faster flash recycling time and are suitable at cold temperatures. Their overall capacity, however, is lower and so they last only for about one third the number of flashes compared with alkaline batteries. Also, since NiCd batteries self-discharge (about 1% per day) at a considerably higher rate than alkaline batteries, I recommend them with reservations. Use only freshly charged nickel-cadmium batteries. Theoretically, modern NiCd batteries are capable of up to 1000 charging cycles when used with a good charging unit. Also, they may be a sensible alternative from an economical, as well as ecological, viewpoint. In practice, though, the capacity of NiCd batteries is reduced significantly due to the so-called "memory effect" after having been used only about 10 to 20 times or even after extended non-use. Cells damaged by this effect can sometimes be regenerated by repeated charge/discharge cycles. Use a charging unit with automatic charge/discharge function ("refresher"). For continuous use, an automatic "maintenance" charge is a good idea.

Tip: The battery of choice for avid flash users.

NiMH (Nickel Metal Hydride) batteries: Advantages of these rechargeable batteries, compared with NiCad batteries, are larger capacity, less self-discharge, and less memory effect. However, they are particularly sensitive to over-charging, so be sure to use charge units specifically designed for NiMH batteries.

Battery Compatibility

Never combine different types of batteries: Due to their different internal resistances, do not mix battery types. Combining alkaline with zinc carbon cells, NiCd, or NiMH batteries may result in rapid destruction of the combined batteries. And, because these combined batteries can also burst and leak, the flash unit could also be seriously damaged!

Risk of Leakage

In normal use, and even in the case of self-discharge during non-use, moisture forms inside the cell. This results in a caustic mixture which, over time, corrodes the battery shell. If this battery fluid reaches the electronic elements of the flash unit, they will be damaged. Considering the external dimensions and the electrical performance, it is technically impossible to manufacture absolutely leak-proof batteries. As far as I know, this has been the reason why battery manufacturers have quietly withdrawn their "leak-proof" guaranties during recent years. As a precaution, because of this risk of leakage, always remove the batteries from the flash unit during extended periods of non-use.

Disposal or Recycling

Only batteries which have been clearly labeled "mercury-free and cadmium-free" should be disposed of as household waste. All batteries, particularly NiCds, should go to recycling centers whenever possible. Some battery manufacturers are beginning to offer this service.

External Power Sources and Accessories

Power bracket SK-6A: This combination of flash unit holder and external battery compartment is described in the section discussing accessories.

Battery pack SD-7: This external battery pack reduces the flash recycling time while increasing the number of flashes by about two to four times. It is used in addition to the alkaline or NiCd batteries present in the flash unit. With the SD-7, you can use the SB-28 successfully in most cold temperatures.

Note: The SD-7 is *not* compatible with the European version of the SB-28.

Battery pack SD-8A: Used along with alkaline or NiCd batteries in

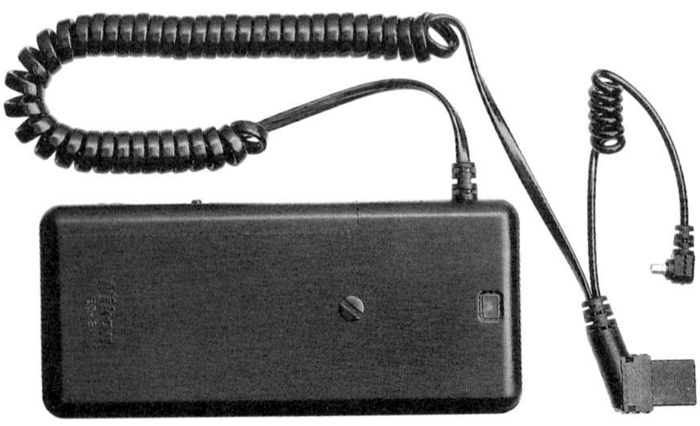

External Battery Pack SD-8

the flash unit, the SD-8A reduces the flash recycling time (with NiCd batteries to approximately two seconds). Also, the SD-8A reduces the recycling time in low temperatures. The SD-8 does not effectively increase the number of flashes as much as the SD-7.

Note: *Only* the SD-8A version is compatible with the European version of the SB-28.

Caution: **Incompatibility of new European versions:** The current international version of the SK-6 is compatible only for use with SB-26, SB-25, SB-24, and SB-22. The European version of the SB-28 requires the new European power bracket, version SK-6A or SD-8A. Due to stricter electrical safety regulations in the EU, the external power sockets of the SB-28 are different from its predecessor models.

Note: It might be worthwhile to contact Nikon to find out whether the old SD-7 or SD-8 may be made compatible by replacing the plug.

Care During Rapid, Consecutive Firing

Excessive, rapid recycling depletes batteries. Rapidly charging the flash capacitor requires considerable electrical energy. This causes the batteries to heat internally, resulting in internal self-discharge and greatly reduced capacity. However, if a period of approximately 30 to 60 seconds elapses between individual flashes, excessive heating does not occur and a greater number of flashes is possible.

Excessive, rapid recycling damages the flash unit. Repeated, rapid, consecutive firing can result in overheating of the flash tube and the flash unit's electronic elements, eventually causing their destruction.

Tip: In general, fire no more than 15 maximum-power flashes consecutively and, whenever the unit becomes warm to touch, take a break for about 10 minutes.

Batteries and Cold Conditions
In cold temperatures, the internal resistance of alkaline batteries rises substantially and the effective capacity drops dramatically. In this case, use only fresh alkaline batteries which have been kept warm, or freshly charged NiCd batteries. For best results, use external battery packs or lithium batteries.

Summary of Battery Recommendations
Combining different types of batteries: Do not combine different types of batteries.

Storage: Cool (but do not freeze) and dry to reduce self-discharge.

Back-up batteries: Even when using rechargeable batteries, it is a good idea to always keep a spare set of fresh batteries.

Care in cold environments: In winter, for example, you should keep spare batteries in a warm, inside pocket of the clothing you are wearing.

Danger of leakage: Always remove batteries from the flash unit during storage or long periods of non-use.

Number of Flashes and Recycling Time as a Function of Power Supply

Type of power source	Rechargeable batteries	Number of flashes * (approx.)	Recycling time (sec.)
Internal	Alkaline/Lithium/NiCd/NiMH	150/200/90/100	6.5s/7.5s/4s/4s
External w/SK-6A	Alkaline/Lithium/NiCd/NiMH	250/300/140/140	4s/4.5s/2.5s/3s
External w/SD-8A	Alkaline/Lithium/NiCd/NiMH	150/350/200/200	3.5s/3.5s/2s/2.5s

**All data apply to an ambient temperature of 68°F (20°C) and greater intervals between flashes. Fast recycling times reduce the number of effective flashes.*

Care of the Flash Unit

Maintenance

Over-cleaning of the flash unit may cause damage. Cleaning the housing with unsuitable fluids–such as acetone, benzene or alcohol solvents–may dissolve it. And cleaning with water could damage the electronics inside. Instead, wipe the housing only with an antistatic cloth, such as Bosch®, and cleaning sprays recommended for electronic units. Never spray cleaner directly on the flash unit. Instead, spray a small amount on a lint-free cloth and then wipe the housing.

Moisture Damage

Moisture and salt water destroy electronic elements: Moisture can be a major problem with the electronics. Modern microprocessors will stop working if the humidity in the surrounding air is too high or if water gets inside the unit. Salt-water spray is particularly corrosive (be careful with ocean mist!) and can easily result in permanent damage.

First aid: Immediately switch off the flash, remove the batteries, and let the unit air-dry.

Precautions: A plastic pouch is ideal to protect your flash unit from rain, excessive air moisture, or when around water. For boating and water sports, water-tight, inflatable, floating containers are recommended. However, condensation can easily form in tight plastic pouches and, as already mentioned, moisture is not good for the electronics. To maintain a dry environment, seal the pouch with a few packets of silica gel inside.

Condensation: Extreme changes in temperature–often caused by going from an outside environment to internal heating or air conditioning, or the reverse–can cause condensation to form on the outside of the flash unit. If this occurs, wipe the surface and leave the unit uncovered until it has air dried. To minimize the chance of condensation occurring when going from one environment to another, keep your camera equipment, including the flash unit, inside your camera bag until all of your gear has reached the surrounding air temperature.

Functional Reliability of the Electrical Components

Cleaning contacts: Unfortunately, the battery compartment and mounting foot of the SB-28 flash unit do not have gold-plated contacts, so normal oxidation is likely to occur. An oxide layer is formed on the contact. This layer can decrease conductivity, even if it is imperceptibly thin. Therefore, from time to time, carefully clean the contacts with a fine pencil eraser.

Refreshing the capacitor during periods of storage: If you intend not to use the flash unit for an extended time, you should still load the batteries and turn the unit on occasionally. After the unit has reached full charge, push the test flash button a few times. Then allow the unit to charge again and, without firing it, switch it off. This procedure refreshes or reforms the flash unit's capacitor and maintains it in good working order. This trick maintains the flash unit's full performance power.

Hands Off the Internal Parts

Modern electronics are not designed for the do-it-yourselfer. If you consider Nikon's service prices too high, you may find the problems caused by you or another untrained person even more costly. *Also, if you allow unauthorized repairs or if you open the flash unit during the warranty period, you will void the standard warranty offered by Nikon.*

The address is "Nikon Service": If your flash requires repair, always send it, carefully packed, to your nearest Nikon authorized service center. Your local photo dealer may be able to help in this regard. Be sure to enclose a copy of your proof of purchase and a detailed description of the problem.

Troubleshooting

Problem

The ready light on the flash does not light up.

Error symptoms: The ready light on the flash unit does not light up even if the unit is switched on, or it goes off again very quickly, or the charging period is considerably longer than 30 seconds.

Check batteries: Are the batteries installed in the unit correctly? Are they depleted? Are they of the same type? To check for depletion, you can use an inexpensive, commercially available battery checker. Or use a voltmeter for a more precise check: A voltage of more than 1.5 volts in each AA cell is quite adequate for alkaline or zinc carbon batteries, as is a voltage above 1.25 volts for NiCd batteries. Fresh batteries should give a reading of 1.55 to 1.65 volts; freshly charged NiCds–1.35 to 1.45 volts. In a pinch, using the trial-and-error method, replace the entire set of batteries with a fresh or freshly charged set. Also remember to clean the battery contacts.

Problem
The bar-shaped distance scale on the LCD of the flash unit disappears or blinks.

Error: This is not a flash unit error but rather a user error. The zoom head may be set for bounce flash or close-up. Unless you intend to use these settings, lock the zoom head in standard position.

Problem
The flash cannot be fired.

Error symptom: Even though the ready light on the flash unit is lit, the camera shutter cannot be released.

Causes: Either there are contact problems or the selected automatic flash features do not work with your camera/lens/flash combination. Even in the case of flash unit or camera processor overload, it's possible for such phenomena to occur.

Contact Problems

Error symptoms: The flash LED (if your camera has one) in the camera viewfinder does not light up, or it flickers. The LCD of the flash unit does not display the expected, required readings. Certain functions of the flash unit–such as the automatic adjustment of the film sensitivity, the zoom head, and the aperture number–do not work. The flash cannot be fired via the camera release even though the ready light on the flash unit is lit.

Check contacts: See the previous section "Functional Reliability of the Electrical Components." It is possible that the battery contacts need cleaning. With F4 and F5 cameras, check to see if the head is properly attached.

Clean flash shoe contacts: The system contacts on the camera mounting shoe should also be gently cleaned from time to time.

Check for correct alignment in the shoe: Regardless of the manufacturer, whenever attaching a flash unit quickly, there seems to be a 50:50 chance that the contacts will align properly. Therefore, take care to insert the flash unit all the way into the camera's shoe until you meet resistance. Then tighten the locking screw without shifting the foot.

Note: The best solution is offered with the N70/F70, N90/F90, and F5 cameras, plus later F4 and N6006/F-601 cameras. In this case, a mount pin on the flash unit engages with a locking recess on the camera shoe.

Problem

The flash unit and camera settings do not match.

Error Symptoms: The flash unit does not perform the way you think it should.

Check flash unit and camera settings: Check whether the desired matching functions are selected on the camera and flash unit. Maybe, in the "heat of battle," you incorrectly changed something. Are you using the camera and lens types which match the desired automatic function?

Example: The film sensitivity transfers automatically to the SB-28 only when used with N90/F90, F4, F5, and N8008/F-801 cameras. The focal length and aperture opening transfer only with AF lenses.

Problem
Overload!

Error symptoms: The flash cannot be triggered from the camera, and/or the flash unit cannot be switched from one function to another. This does not include errors listed previously.

Causes of overload: Electrostatic charges or signals which do not meet the standard for voltage or timing may occasionally get out of control in microprocessor-controlled cameras and flash units. (This is not a problem exclusive to Nikon.)

Camera overload: The shutter cannot be released even after removing the flash unit; the LCD blinks "senselessly;" operating modes cannot be reversed; the camera can no longer be switched off with the main switch; or the mirror does not return to its resting position.

Recommendation: Move the main switch to "Off" and remove the batteries from the camera for a few minutes. (This allows the camera's microprocessor, which has been blocked by error information, to discharge electrically so that it is again ready for operation.) Your camera should function again after two or three tries. If these phenomena occur frequently, however, it is likely that a chip is defective and you should have the camera serviced by Nikon.

Flash unit overload: Switch off the camera. Then switch off the flash unit and remove it from the camera. After remounting and reactivating the flash unit, you should be able to again switch between operating modes.

Power overload: If you have connected too many flash units with each other in TTL-controlled multiple flash mode, it's possible that a second flash burst cannot be fired. Disconnect the main unit from the camera, switch off all the flash units, then reconnect and switch them on again. If necessary, use one less flash unit.

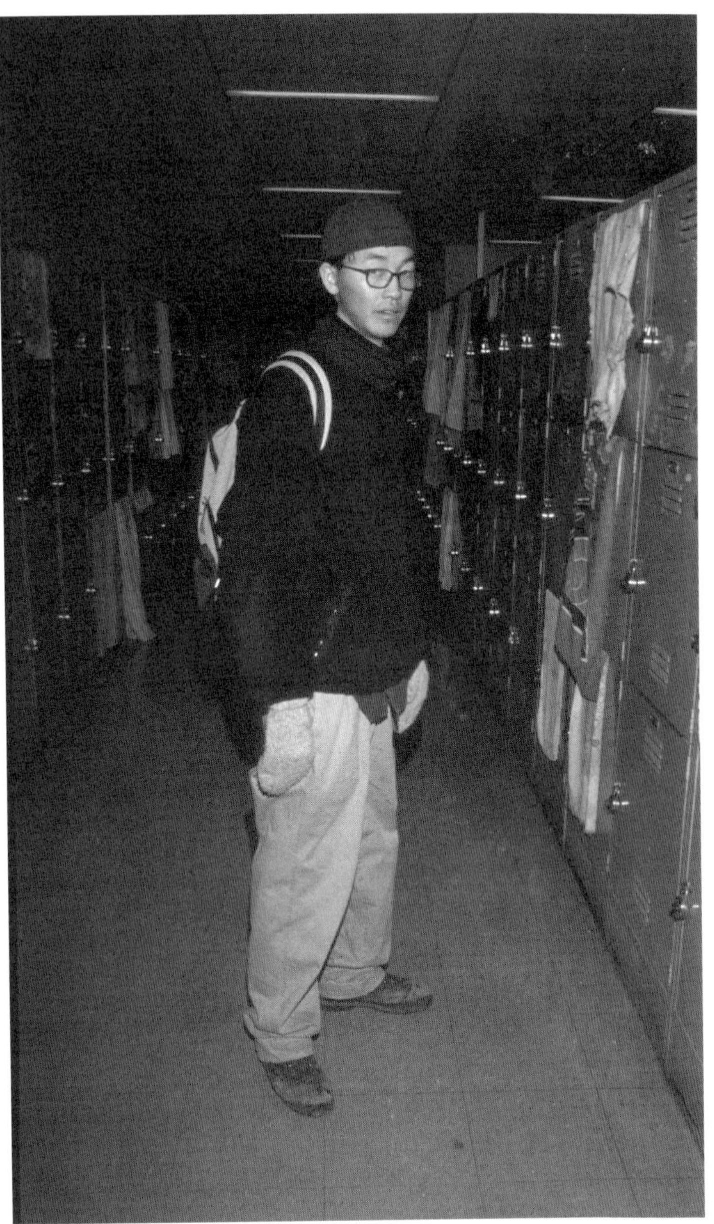

Flash Control Features

Flash ready indicators: If the ready light on the flash unit and/or flash LED in the camera viewfinder have been lit for at least two seconds, the flash unit is charged and ready for firing. Do not be misled by consecutive firing: You may trigger a flash immediately after the LED lights up; however, the unit's power may not yet be at 100% capacity.

Confusing existing-light readout: In some cameras, such as the N8008/F-801 and N90/F90, the ambient-light exposure, as well as the automatic read-out for shutter speed and aperture, are shown when using TTL autoflash. If the readout indicates over- or underexposure, it refers strictly to the ambient exposure. If underexposure is indicated, and that area also will receive flash exposure, the resulting image may be acceptable. However, the over- or underexposure warning indicates that existing light may not have been given proper consideration. For the best TTL fill-flash results, use matrix metering and automatic exposure; or use spot or center-weighted metering and selectively measure a specific area to establish a basic existing-light exposure. Then set the camera manually. Or if in autoexposure, press and hold the AE-L (automatic exposure lock) button to lock-in the exposure before recomposing. Release the AE-L button after shooting.

Flash exposure control: If the flash ready light or the flash LED in the camera viewfinder blinks several times after firing, the flash was probably too weak. There are several causes for this: The subject was beyond the distance range; the film sensitivity was too low, or, depending on the automatic features, the aperture opening was insufficient. In this case, underexposed pictures will probably result. The solutions are to use a closer flash-to-subject distance, faster film, or larger (wider) aperture opening.

< Use TTL autoflash with aperture priority mode to limit background brightness, such as down this hall.

Underexposure indication in f/stops (N70/F70, F5, N90/F90): When using the N90/F90 camera, the flash LCD may indicate an underexposure in TTL-controlled flash mode up to -3 EV in 0.3 f/stops. If you see this, select a wider aperture or move closer.

"HI" indication: The overexposure indication "HI," which appears in the viewfinder of the camera, applies only to the ambient-light reading. This generally indicates (usually in situations where back-lighting is present) that the background will be too light due to the limitations of the flash sync speed. However, the foreground, which has been lit by the flash, should be correctly exposed assuming that it isn't also illuminated by the same level of ambient light.

Improper contact: If the contact between the flash unit and the mounting shoe is not stable, the flash indicator diode in the camera viewfinder may blink or will not stay lit.

Test flash: You can fire the flash on the SB-28 without exposing the film by manually triggering the unit. A test flash is not appraised by the TTL metering system in the camera; it is only read by the sensor built into the flash unit. If the ready light on the flash unit does not flash after a test flash, the flash output will probably be sufficient for good exposure. If you are using TTL mode, you must switch to "A" to operate the test flash feature.

Flash Methods and Applications

The SB-28 features three standard flash modes: TTL autoflash ("TTL"), non-TTL automatic flash ("A"), and manual flash ("M"). In addition, there are two special flash functions–stroboscopic flash (multiple flash symbol) and high-speed synchronization ("FP"). Additional auxiliary features allow optional synchronization with the first or second shutter curtain, red-eye reduction, monitor pre-flash, and 3D matrix, or multi-sensor or matrix-controlled automatic fill-flash in TTL autoflash mode. The mode you choose depends on the capabilities of your camera, the subject, and specific picture-taking conditions.

Ultimately, of course, the quality of the finished photo is the most important criterion. The following chapters provide help in selecting the best method for a given subject and anticipated result. An explanation of actual flash methods will be followed by a discussion of suggested combinations for use with the automatic exposure features of various cameras.

Classic, Fully Manual Flash

Principle

The photographer computes the correct aperture for the subject distance and film speed, or takes a flash meter reading and adjusts the aperture accordingly. The flash unit, itself, works with a default guide number (or optionally, the SB-28 also works with a reduced guide number, see the following).

Suitable Cameras and Lenses

The SB-28 will operate in manual flash mode with all Nikon cameras and lenses. Adapters are available if your camera is not equipped with a hot shoe.

Note: The following explanations apply only to the SB-28 when it is attached to a camera. Different rules apply to flash exposures taken in the studio where the work is principally manual and the flash units are separated from the camera. (See the section "Studio Flash Photography.")

LCD using manual flash mode.

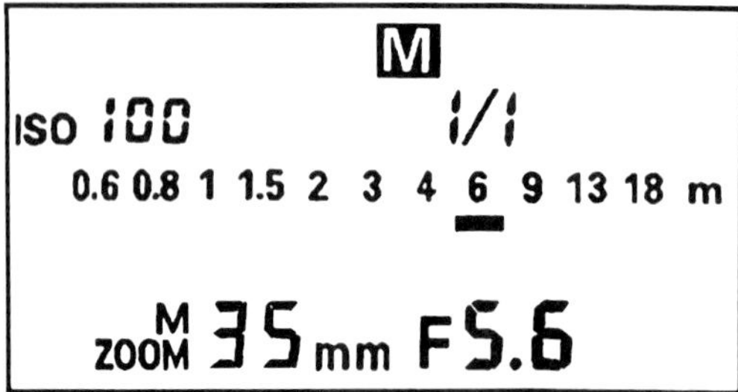

Procedure

- Mount the SB-28 to the camera accessory shoe and turn on the camera and flash.
- Set the ISO film speed on the SB-28 (within 5 seconds).
- Select "M" mode on the SB-28.
- Set the SB-28's zoom head for the focal length of the lens.
- If necessary, set the camera to flash sync speed.
- Focus on your subject.
- Adjust the aperture (using the "SEL" and plus/minus buttons) on the flash unit until the distance indicated on the SB-28's LCD corresponds to the subject distance.
- Adjust the aperture on the camera lens until it corresponds to that indicated on the SB-28.
- Press the shutter release.
- For flash control options, see "Flash Control Features" in the chapter *Using the SB-28.*

With practice, you should be able to perform the above steps quickly.

Cameras with TTL dedication: For cameras with dedicated TTL flash capability, the shutter speed of the camera is adjusted automatically to the correct flash sync speed. Other than that, proceed as described above.

Using N8008/F-801, F4, N70/F70, F4, F5, N90/F90 cameras with manual flash: The film sensitivity and zoom head are adjusted automatically on these cameras. Also the selected aperture settings are automatically relayed from the camera to the flash.

- Set the camera on manual exposure or aperture priority and select an appropriate flash sync speed up to 1/250 second.
- Focus on your subject.
- In manual flash mode, the LCD panel will "receive" the aperture settings from the camera automatically.

Limits of manual flash photography: When using just the guide-number calculation, perfect flash exposures are almost always an exception. This is because the effective guide number fluctuates slightly as a function of flash recycling time, and also because ambient light and subject characteristics play an important role in the overall exposure. Manual flash exposures using a flash exposure meter are more reliable.

Note: The SB-28 indicates aperture readings only in whole stops. You can make intermediate lens aperture settings by fine-tuning the flash guide number on the flash unit (see below).

Bracket your exposures: When using manual flash, is best to make a series of bracketed exposures over and under the calculated exposure.

Selection of aperture and distance by varying the flash power output: In manual mode, the guide number predetermines the aperture for a given distance from the subject. This is not always ideal from an artistic viewpoint. Because the SB-28 allows you to reduce the power output in 7 steps in 1/3-f/stop increments (using the plus/minus buttons), aperture and distance may be varied within a wide range. For example, if the 1/1 (full) output level requires f/8 for a distance of 13 feet, pictures may be taken at 1/4 power using f/4, and at 1/8 power using f/2.8. Conversely, if you want to maintain a desired aperture and get closer to the subject, use the power output feature to adjust for the distance change. For example, if the appropriate subject distance is 13 feet, with a constant aperture of f/8 and an output level of 1/1 (or full), it is possible to move to 2 feet with an output level of 1/64.

Precise adjustment of power output: When using manual flash, it is possible with any camera to fine-tune the power output of the SB-28 in 1/3-f/stop increments from 1/2 to 1/64. This option is in addition to the output levels 1/1 (full) to 1/64 and different from the SB-25 and the SB-26. If you are attempting a series of finely tuned flash exposures or transferring values from a sensitive handheld flash meter, you'll find that this method is significantly more accurate than adjusting the lens aperture. The latter should be set at a full value with the fine adjustment performed on the flash unit.

Manual flash with automatic flash sync: Effectively, this does no more than manual flash exposure. The only difference is that the shutter speed is automatically set for flash sync on cameras featuring this option. In some cameras which use matrix, center-weighted, or spot metering, the flash synchronization speed is varied automatically between 1/60 and 1/250 second to match the ambient light and the selected aperture. (In slow sync, these cameras can chose between 30 seconds and 1/250 second).

Manual Mode

In some cases manual mode is better than TTL autoflash mode: It has been my experience with the SB-24, SB-25, SB-26, and SB-28 that precisely adjusted manual flash is sometimes better than standard TTL autoflash exposure. (Even exposures using a matrix-balanced automatic flash are sometimes only equally as good as those made with manual flash).

All subjects exhibiting high or unusual reflectance require careful evaluation with the use of standard TTL autoflash or even matrix-balanced fill-flash. Of course, the best solution is 3D multi-sensor balanced fill-flash with monitor preflash and type D lens distance information. Compared with this, manual flash photography no longer offers any advantages.

Manual Flash With Motor Drives or Winders

Autoflash modes are less suitable for continuous exposures: Due to longer flash recycling times, automatic flash modes are less suitable for continuous exposures. The risk that the flash may fail at precisely the most important moment because its capacitor is not fully charged, is simply too great.

Caution: The SB-28 may overheat; therefore, in "A" and "TTL" modes no more than 15 flashes may be fired continuously.

Manual flash mode for continuous exposures: For quick recycling during continuous exposures, select manual mode on the SB-28 and reduce the power output (between 1/8 and 1/64). In most cases, shorter subject distances and/or larger aperture openings must be used to accommodate this reduced output. The number of flashes able to be fired continuously are limited by the back-up capacity of the power supply and the risk of the SB-28 overheating. In any event, a fresh set of alkaline batteries or freshly charged NiCds will allow the continuous firing of up to 30 exposures at 1/64 power and up to 4 exposures at 1/8 power at a rate of up to 6 exposures per second. By using external power pack SD-8A or SK-6A, the number of flashes may be increased.

Non-TTL Automatic Mode "A"

Principle

The duration of the flash is controlled independently from the camera's electronic system via a sensor on the flash unit. In this case, the sensor measures the light reflected off the subject during an exposure. The photographer may select any aperture covered by the range of the flash. (The SB-28 makes the choice of aperture very easy; many other flash units are more complicated.) For additional information, see the chapter *The Basics of Flash Technology.*

Suitable Cameras and Lenses

On fully manual cameras and lenses, or even with cameras featuring automatic exposure, the SB-28 may be used in non-TTL automatic flash mode "A." Appropriate adapters are available if your camera does not have a hot shoe with the ISO sync contact.

LCD using non-TTL automatic flash mode "A."

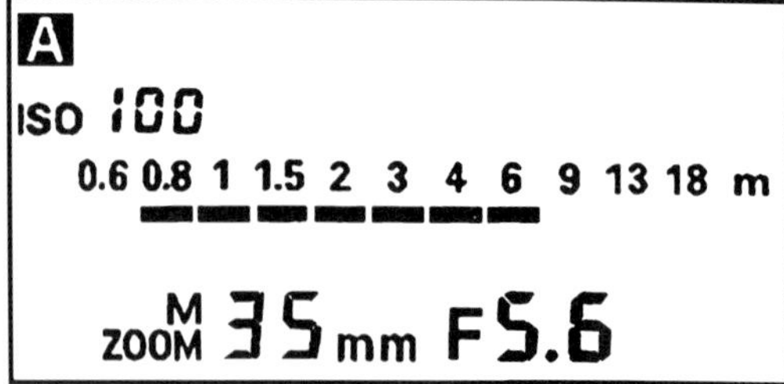

Procedure

- Mount the SB-28 in the camera accessory shoe and switch on the camera and the flash.
- Set the film speed on the SB-28 (within 5 seconds).
- Set the SB-28 to "A" mode.
- Set the SB-28's zoom head for the focal length of the lens in use.
- If necessary, set the camera to flash sync speed.
- Focus on your subject.
- Set the desired aperture on the camera lens.
- Also set this aperture on the LCD of the SB-28 and verify that the distance range covers the focus distance on the lens.
- Optionally, change the aperture on the lens *and* flash unit until the proper distance range is reached.
- All you need to do now is press the shutter release.
- For flash controls see "Flash Control Features" in the chapter *Using the SB-28.*

Cameras with TTL flash capability: In cameras which are already equipped with dedicated TTL flash, the shutter speed of the camera is adjusted automatically to the flash sync speed when "A" mode is used. Other than that, you should follow the procedure described above.

Using N8008/F-801, N70/F70, F4, F5, and N90/F90 cameras: The ISO film speed and zoom head are automatically adjusted in these cameras. The flash sync speed may be selected freely up to 1/250 second.

- Set the camera for manual exposure and select an appropriate flash sync speed.

- Focus on your subject.
- Adjust the aperture on the SB-28 flash unit until the distance indicated on the SB-28's LCD corresponds to the distance setting on the camera.
- Adjust the aperture setting on the camera lens until it corresponds with setting indicated on the flash unit's LCD.

When to Use Non-TTL Automatic Mode "A"

Generally inferior to manual or TTL autoflash modes: In complex cases, a precisely adjusted manual flash exposure is better than non-TTL automatic flash. Also, because the measured angle remains the same (the flash sensor in "A" mode is not matched to the angle of coverage of the lens) and the controllable range is smaller, it is generally inferior to TTL autoflash modes.

When "A" mode is the best alternative: Use the non-TTL automatic flash "A" when your camera doesn't have TTL autoflash and "grabbing the shot" is a higher priority than perfect exposures. The advantage of the SB-28 over other automatic flash units (depending on the film sensitivity) is an aperture range of up to 7 steps and a distance range of 2 to 54 feet (0.6 to 18 m).

TTL Flash—More Convenience and Reliability

Even though, at first glance, the variety of TTL flash modes offered by the SB-28 appears confusing, the user is supported quite well when selecting the flash mode. With classic cameras using a TTL flash sensor, the SB-28 permits only conventional TTL autoflash (display: "TTL" only). For use with modern cameras without matrix metering, the SB-28 offers TTL auto fill-flash in addition to conventional TTL autoflash. On modern AF-cameras with matrix metering, the SB-28 may even be switched to matrix-balanced TTL auto fill-flash. Also, depending on lens and camera capabilities, the monitor preflash, the flash multi-sensor, and 3-D matrix-metering may be used.

Standard TTL Autoflash "TTL"

Principle

After triggering the shutter release, light reflected off the film during the flash exposure is measured (with a slight emphasis on the center) by a sensor in the bottom of the camera. The duration of the flash is adjusted to achieve a middle-value exposure. Unlike TTL auto fill-flash mode, there is no automatic adjustment of the flash duration (or as Nikon prefers, no automatic "compensation"). Additional information is provided in the chapter *The Basics of Flash Technology.* Handling is relatively simple; the photographer selects an aperture appropriate for the distance range.

Suitable Cameras and Lenses

For almost all current Nikon cameras: The SB-28 can be used with standard TTL autoflash with almost all Nikon cameras featuring TTL flash control. An exception is the F3 camera which has the TTL flash option only when used with certain "F3 flash units." Depending on the camera model, TTL autoflash can be combined with manual or automatic camera exposure modes. TTL autoflash can be used with practically all lenses.

Normal, main subject surrounded by an area of high and low reflectance: These pictures were taken with an N90/F90 camera and an AF-D Nikkor lens. The 3D matrix-controlled TTL multi-sensor auto fill-flash works well in spite of the relatively tiny main subject and the unusual reflectance of the surroundings. In both cases, an exposure with zero correction is still acceptable. The best exposure of the main subject was obtained with exposure corrections of approximately -0.7 with black surroundings and +0.7 with white surroundings. ➢

Autoflash comparison: Here variations in subject size and position against a dark background were used to illustrate the result of different cameras and flash methods with the SB-28 flash. The N90/F90 camera with 3D-multi-sensor auto fill-flash with a type-D AF Nikkor lens yields good results (top) with well-exposed skin tones. The N90/F90's 3D autoflash with a normal AF Nikkor lens (second row) also yields good results. The N8008/F-801's TTL matrix auto fill-flash without multi-sensor (third row) resulted in washed-out skin tones. The N2000/F-301's conventional TTL autoflash (fourth row) also produced overexposed skin tones. ➢➢

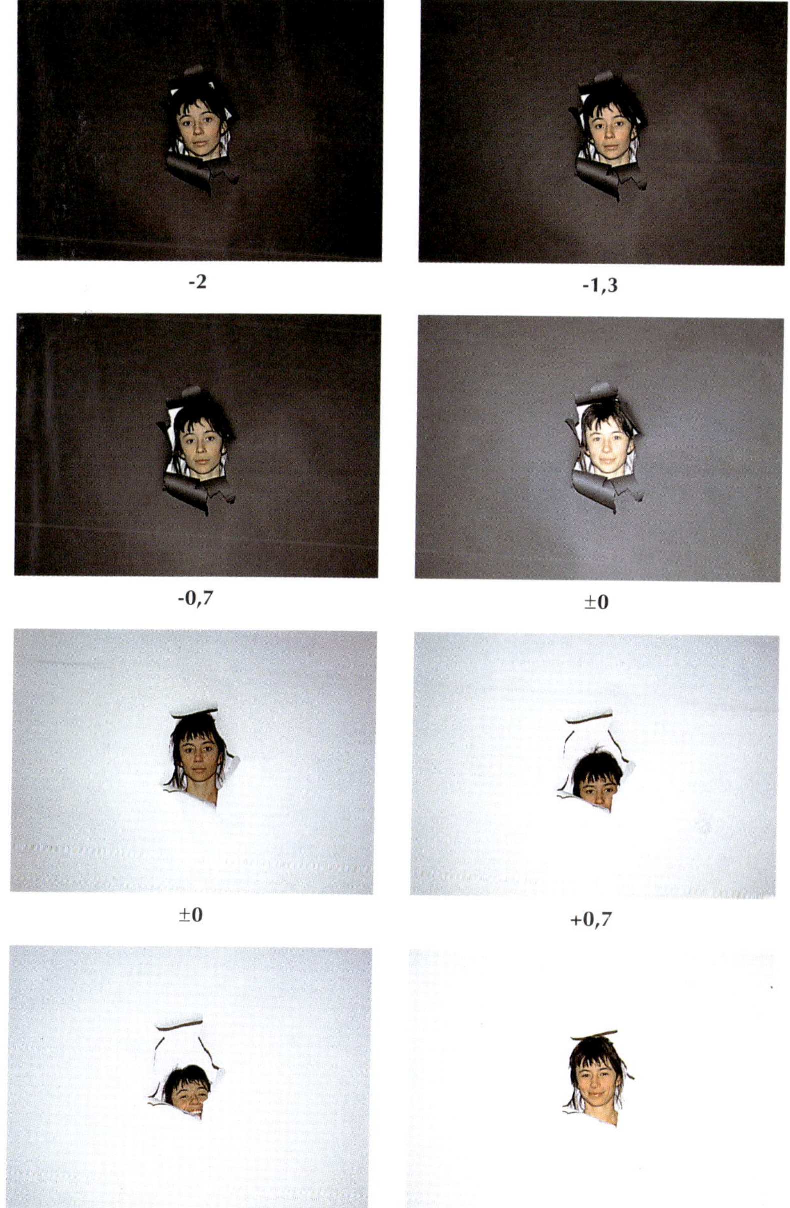

-2 -1,3

-0,7 ±0

±0 +0,7

+1,3 +2

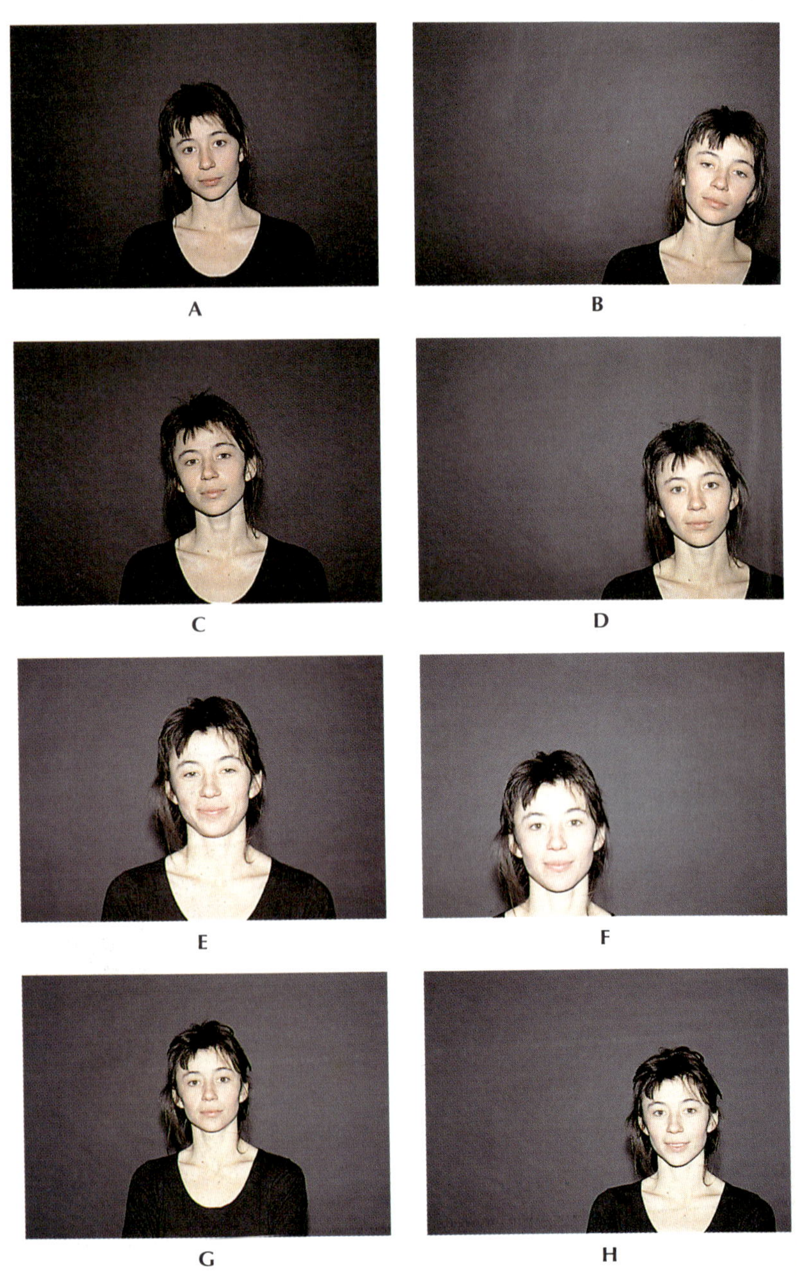

A B C D E F G H

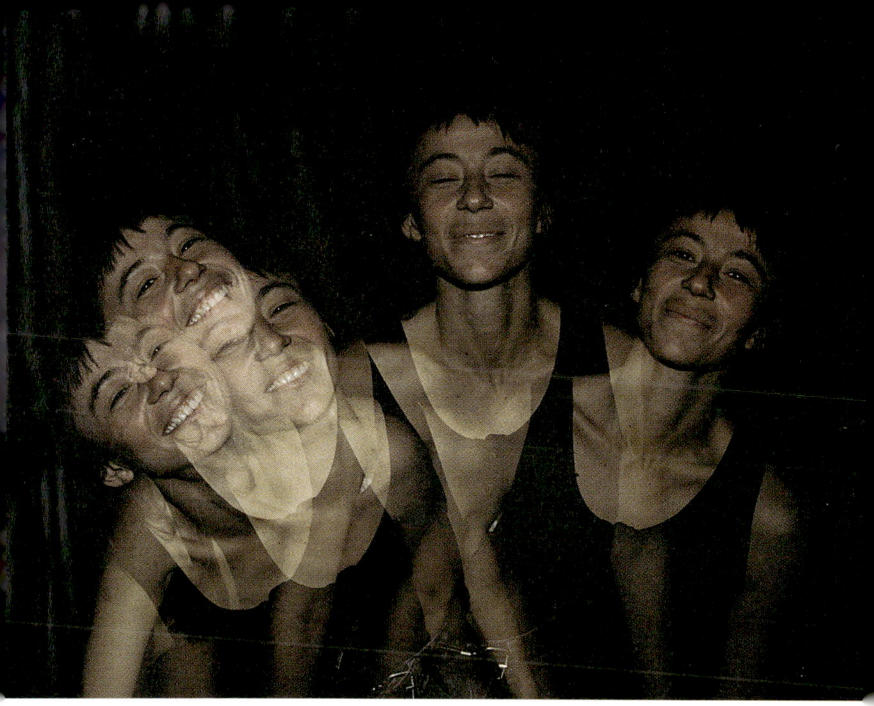

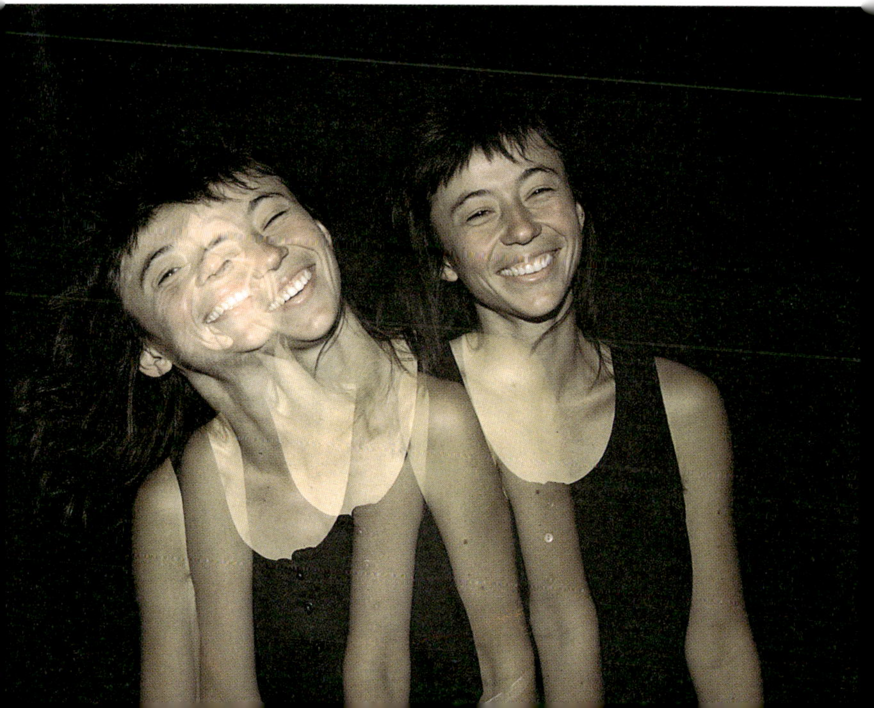

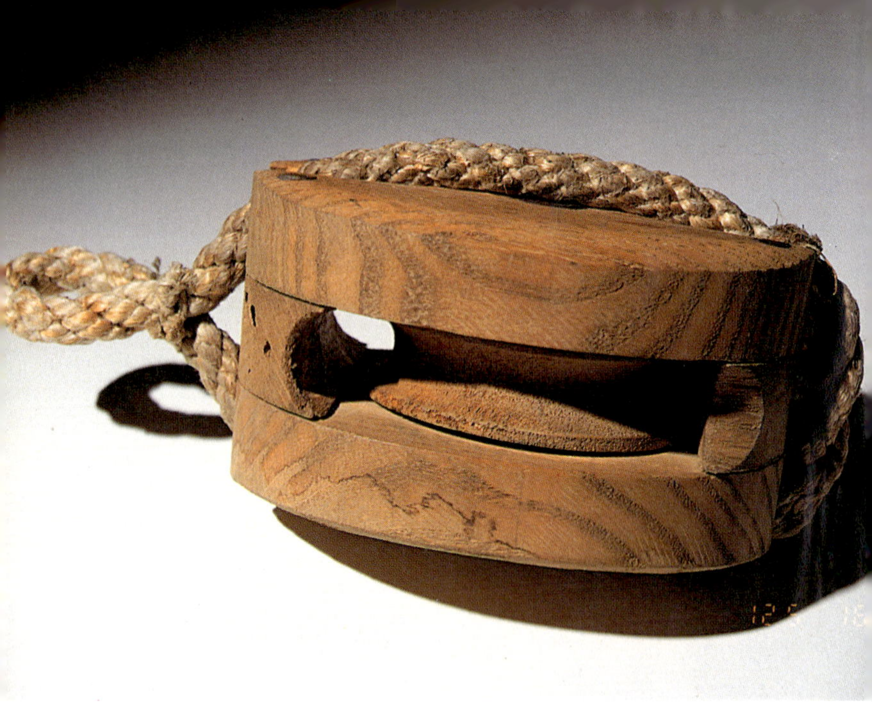

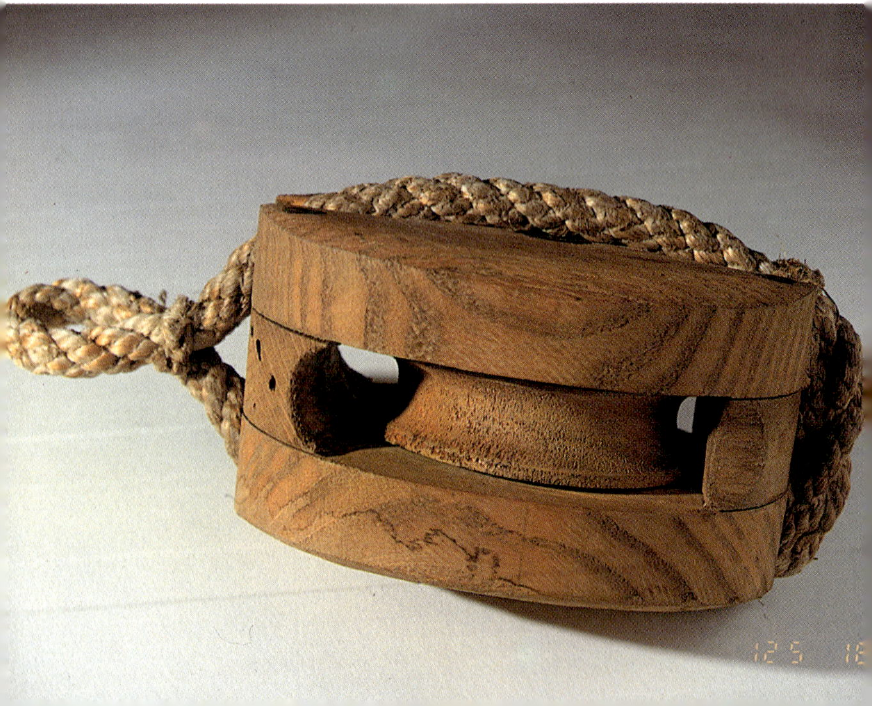

LCD using standard TTL autoflash mode.

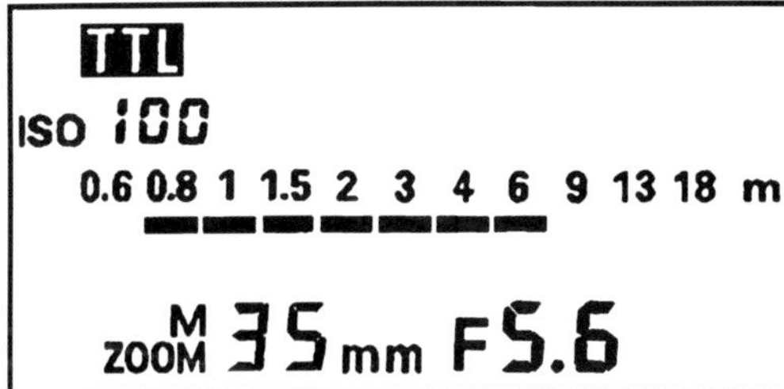

Procedure

- Mount the SB-28 to the camera accessory shoe and switch on the camera and flash.
- Set the correct film speed on the SB-28 (within 5 seconds).
- Set the SB-28 on "TTL" mode.
- If necessary, set the SB-28's zoom head to the desired focal length.
- Select any exposure mode on the camera (manual, auto, or even programmed exposure).
- If necessary, set the camera to flash sync speed.
- Focus on your subject.
- If using "M" or "A" camera exposure mode, select the desired aperture on the camera lens.

Stroboscopic flash exposures: These exposures were made in total darkness against a black background, with a sequence of five and three flash exposures, respectively. In areas where several images overlap, a partial overexposure is noticeable, while other areas appear even somewhat underexposed. It's a good idea to make trial exposures prior to taking serious pictures using the stroboscopic flash mode.

Studio-type illumination with only one flash: These exposures were made with the N90/F90 camera and an AF-D Nikkor lens in 3D-TTL multi-sensor fill-flash mode using manual exposure (f/16 and 1/125 second). One SB-28 was used. It was placed diagonally from the top left front at a distance of about three feet from the main subject. The subject size was six inches. The zoom head was set for 20mm (with the wide-angle panel). The flash was aligned with a home-made modeling light. The high-contrast picture was made with only one flash modifier (a white reflector, approximately 20 inches to the right of the subject). The soft-contrast picture was made with a diffuser card, plus tracing paper positioned halfway between the SB-28 and the subject.

- If necessary, set this aperture on the LCD of the SB-28 and check whether the displayed distance range matches the focused distance on the lens.
- If necessary, adjust the aperture on the lens *and* flash unit it correlates with the distance range.
- All you need to do now is press the shutter release.
- For flash controls, see "Flash Control Features" in the chapter *Using the SB-28.*

Older cameras using programmed exposure modes: When programmed exposure modes are used, the camera selects a fixed flash sync speed and, depending on the camera model, a fixed aperture (or the latter is varied automatically as a function of ambient light measurement).

Standard TTL Autoflash

In complex lighting conditions, a precisely adjusted, fully manual flash exposure may be better than a standard TTL autoflash exposure. This is because the absence of a monitor preflash makes standard TTL flash inferior to the auto fill-flash modes, in particular, those using matrix-metering.

Cameras without advanced TTL autoflash fill-flash capability: In this situation, matrix-controlled or "standard" TTL auto fill-flash will be used if the camera does not offer another choice.

Fill-flash with older, classic cameras: Even older cameras, such as the N2000/F-301, N2020/F-501, and FA, are capable of acceptable fill-flash exposures with manual ambient-light exposure adjustment. For minus corrections, simply set the ISO film speed higher than the one actually in use.

TTL Automatic Fill-Flash

Principle

This automatic mode, in its simplest form, merely represents an automatically determined flash compensation. Ambient light is measured using a center-weighted bias. However, the background is generally not given enough emphasis or consideration. Advanced auto fill-flash systems more accurately account for ambient light or the brightness of the background. For additional information regarding this method, see the chapter *The Basics of Flash Technology.*

Concept

Conventional Cameras: All models use center-weighted measurement of the flash reflected by the subject. Also, continuous light is center-weighted. The SB-28 permits only "TTL" setting. (See "Standard TTL Flash.") Therefore, an automatic consideration of existing light during flash exposure is not possible.

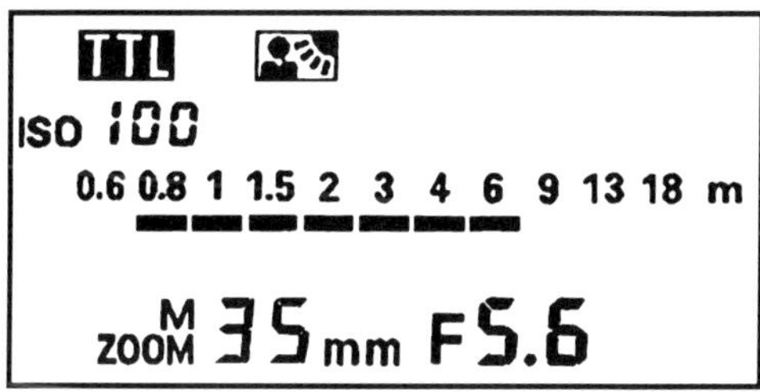

LCD using TTL auto fill-flash. The fill-flash symbol appears whenever automatic fill-flash is used with TTL flash control, which slightly reduces the flash exposure. This does not affect the camera's ambient metering system (matrix, center-weighted, or spot).

Modern Cameras: When matrix-metering is used, ambient light must not only be measured in several segments but a mathematical matrix will be used to evaluate absolute brightness and contrast. As a rule, this matrix is active only with AF-lenses. As usual, the flash is measured center-weighted in an integral manner. In addition to the "TTL" setting, the SB-28 sets the TTL fill-flash. The symbol, which is displayed on the LCD for this setting in addition to the TTL symbol, depends on the camera/lens combination and is not quite logical for all possible combinations.

Cameras featuring multi-segment, center-weighted, and spot-metering: In ambient light, cameras such as the N6006/F-601, N8008s/F-801s, N70/F70, N90/F90, and F5 may be switched from multi-segment to center-weighted metering, sometimes even to spot-metering. In this case, the center-weighted or spot-metering value is used for correcting the TTL flash exposure in TTL automatic fill-flash mode. Readings for auto fill-flash on the SB-28's LCD do not change when changing the exposure method on the camera.

Non-AF Nikkor lenses on modern cameras using matrix-metering: Modern cameras do not permit matrix-metering, only center-weighted metering. In this situation, you can switch the SB-28 from conventional TTL autoflash to TTL automatic fill-flash. Depending on the camera type, the fill-flash symbol appears next to the TTL symbol on the SB-28's display. (In the case of cameras offering flash mode switching capability on the camera, e.g., the N6006/F-601, only the TTL symbol remains on the display.) This situation represents one which could be described appropriately as "TTL automatic fill-flash" with the use of Nikon cameras in combination with the SB-25, SB-26, or SB-28.

Advanced cameras with TTL flash-multi-sensor: These cameras always use the multi-sensor for TTL flash-metering, i.e., AF- or non-AF-Nikkor lenses. When TTL automatic fill-flash is activated on the SB-28 and cameras such as the N90/F90 are used, the matrix symbol will appear with AF Nikkor lenses and the fill-flash symbol will appear with non-AF Nikkor lenses.

TTL Automatic Fill-Flash as Emergency Solution for Non-AF Lenses

TTL automatic fill-flash mode represents only an emergency solution, permitting automatic fill-flash when a few select, modern Nikon cameras are used with non-AF-lenses. To obtain natural-looking pictures, center-weighted TTL automatic fill-flash should be used in manual exposure setting mode for optimum integration of the background.

Spot, Center-Weighted TTL Flash for Background Brightness Correction

On occasion, experienced photographers using advanced cameras, such as the N90/F90 or F5 with AF-lenses, switch from matrix-metering to spot-metering or center-weighted metering in ambient light. This allows optimal background illumination. In addition, foreground flash exposure can be enhanced by manual flash corrections on the SB-28 itself.

Tip: When using the N90/F90 or F5, make some test exposures first to help you achieve an improvement over the automatic settings.

Matrix-Balanced TTL Automatic Fill-Flash

Principle

This flash mode automatically considers ambient light (and in the case of backlit subjects, the contrast relative to the background brightness) based on matrix metering. This is done before the actual flash exposure. The auto system sets the flash sync speed and aperture appropriate for the ambient light. The TTL sensor controls the flash during the exposure based on a slightly center-weighted evaluation. When the shutter is released, a precise adjustment takes place based on the TTL-sensor which monitors the actual exposure.

Suitable Cameras and Lenses

N6006/F-601, N8008/F-801, N70/F70, F4, and N90/F90: With AF Nikkor lenses, these cameras work with matrix metering when set on "Matrix" in program exposure with matrix-balanced TTL fill-flash. You can use semi-automatic camera exposure modes; however, you won't achieve the full automatic control range of shutter speed and aperture.

Note: Depending on the camera, the fill-flash symbol may or may not appear on the SB-28's LCD along with the "TTL" symbol (for example, no symbol with the N6006/F-601; fill-flash symbol with the N8008/F-801; matrix symbol with the N90/F90).

Procedure

- Mount the SB-28 in the camera accessory shoe and switch on both the camera and flash.
- Set the SB-28 on "TTL" mode or, depending on the camera model, on the TTL symbol with the additional fill-flash or matrix symbol.
- Film speed and zoom head are set automatically (not on the N6006/F-601).
- Select an automatic exposure mode or manual exposure setting.
- With manual exposure and shutter priority setting, a flash synchronization speed up to 1/250 second (1/125 second on the N6006/F-601) can be selected depending on the camera model.
- The aperture value will be transferred automatically to the SB-28 (not with the N6006/F-601).
- Focus on your subject.
- Check whether the distance range displayed by the flash unit's LCD is appropriate for the distance to the subject. If necessary, adjust the aperture on the lens (or first the automatic mode) until it is appropriate for the indicated distance range.
- Press the shutter release.
- For further information, see "Flash Control Features" in the chapter *Using the SB-28.*

Matrix-Balanced Automatic Fill-Flash

The best flash method with advanced cameras: For normal photography, I cannot think of a better flash method than matrix metering with automatic exposure.

Enhanced automatic capabilities with N70/F70, N90/F90, and F5 cameras: With AF-lenses, the SB-28 provides improved auto fill-flash plus additional monitor preflash, TTL multi-sensor metering, and 3D matrix for controlled fine-tuning. See the following section for a more detailed explanation of these advanced automatic flash modes.

Caution with difficult subjects: Subjects exhibiting extremes of reflectance or lack of reflectance (black on black or white on white) or subjects that are off-center, can cause exposure problems. In these cases, manual metering and manual flash exposure with additional adjustments often yield better results.

Backlit exposures with fill-flash: If you photograph a subject in front of a light background using matrix metering and standard TTL flash without fill-flash, it usually reproduces lighter than the background. Pictures taken with automatic exposure compensation are frequently too light or the background is unnaturally light and colors in the subject are poorly saturated due to excessive illumination. In contrast, by using automatic fill-flash, the subject's colors are saturated and the background is rendered at a normal brightness level.

Avoiding overexposure of surrounding images with matrix control: Often, in flash photography, you can create a pleasant mood if the surrounding area is not overexposed by the flash. Overexposure can be prevented by using auto fill-flash mode. This brightens the image in a subtle manner by combining a relatively high exposure (large aperture and relatively slow shutter speed) with a low-power flash (automatic minus correction).

TTL Multi-Sensor Auto Fill-Flash

Principle

As in normal, matrix-balanced TTL fill-flash mode, the aperture, shutter speed, and duration of the flash are adjusted before the shutter release is pressed. This is based on a measurement of ambient light and, possibly, subject contrast. After firing the flash, TTL control is also based on multi-segment/multi-sensor metering and the same evaluation of brightness distribution. Deviations from preliminary settings (e.g., monitor preflash not activated due to tilted zoom head) will be corrected by the duration of the flash.

Suitable Cameras and Lenses

Presently all AF and non-AF lenses can be used with N70/F70, N90/F90, and F5 cameras.

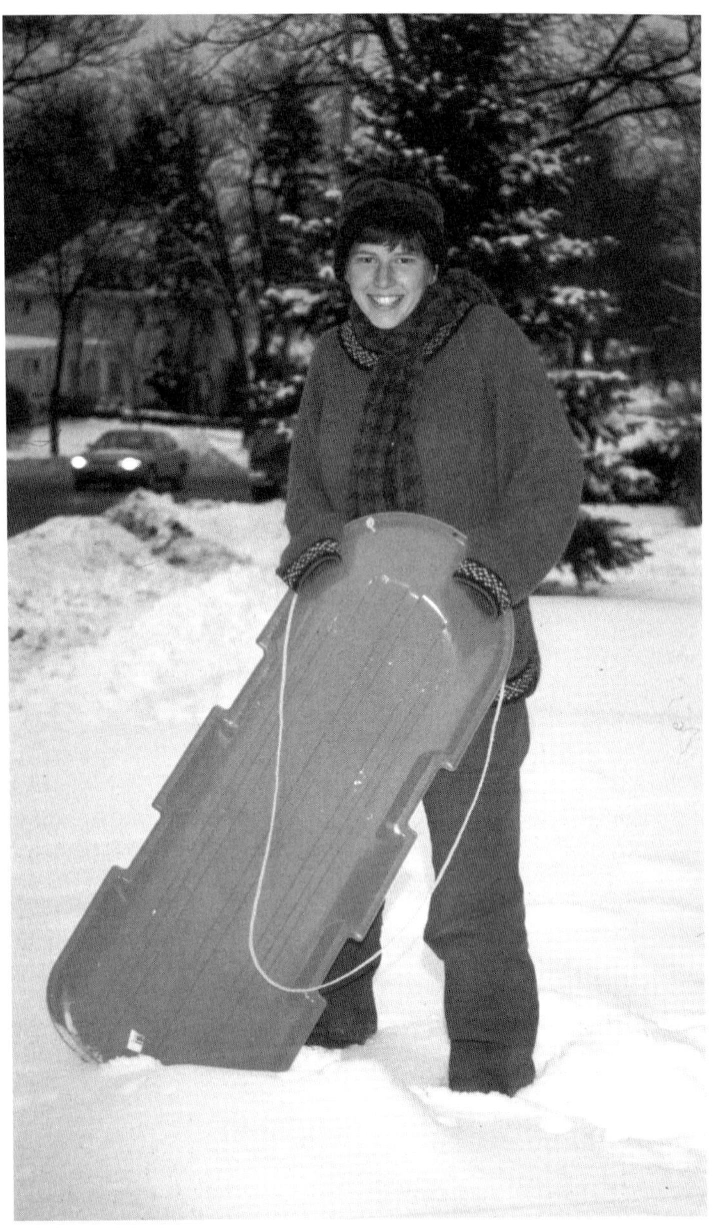

LCD using TTL multi-sensor auto fill-flash mode. The displayed symbol appears only with the use of AF-cameras, such as the N90/F90, N70/F70, and F5, and activated matrix TTL multi-sensor auto fill-flash. If a non-AF lens is used, the matrix symbol will be replaced by the fill-flash symbol.

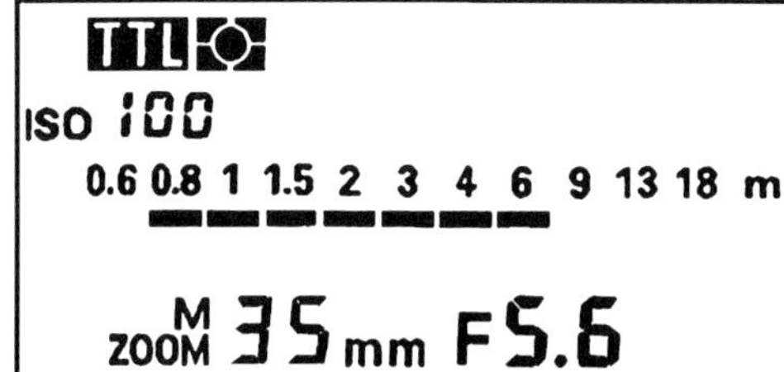

Note: Nikon is not very clear concerning the response with the use of non-AF lenses. The current SB-28 user manual refers to "switching TTL flash metering from multi-sensor to center-weighted" and to "... if AF lenses are not used, ... center-weighted exposures are obtained (thanks to multi-sensor)." I was able to clarify with Nikon that with the use of the N90/F90 and SB-26, with non-AF lenses, matrix-metering of ambient light is no longer possible. Instead, use center-weighted metering (or spot-metering). Still, monitor preflash and multi-sensor are used for flash fine-tuning and produce significantly improved flash exposures with non-AF lenses.

Procedure

- To be activated, the zoom head must not be tilted. (Lock in normal, forward position.)
- If off-camera flash is used, flash range and flash angle may differ significantly from the camera location. Then metering with the monitor preflash may be completely out of range. ***Note:*** For monitor preflash to be activated, the flash head must be in the normal, forward position. If the head is bounced, swiveled, or tilted, the automatic preflash will be canceled.
- Appropriate cameras activate the monitor preflash automatically.
- Appropriate cameras activate the multi-sensor automatically.

< Auto fill-flash mode was used for this photo taken at dusk. The aperture/shutter speed combination recorded the waning ambient light, and the low-power flash illuminated the subject without overexposing the snowy winter scene.

- For other settings, see conventional or matrix-controlled TTL auto fill-flash.

When to Use TTL Multi-Sensor Auto Fill-Flash

With appropriate cameras and a setting of "TTL" + "fill-flash" on the SB-28, this function is activated automatically. Actually, pictures of all subjects in all situations benefit from this.

Note: With non-AF lenses, the SB-28 displays the fill-flash symbol. With AF lenses, the matrix symbol is displayed.

3D Matrix TTL Fill-Flash

Principle

In this case, the use of AF Nikkor type D lenses activates an additional distance adjustment relative to the main subject and uses it in the preliminary flash correction. (See the chapter *The Basics of Flash Technology.*)

Suitable Cameras and Lenses

This mode is available *only* when N70/F70, N90/F90, and F5 cameras are used with AF Nikkor type D lenses.

Procedure

- The 3D matrix is activated automatically when AF-D Nikkor lenses are used.
- Otherwise, proceed as with matrix-balanced auto fill-flash.

When to Use 3D Matrix TTL Auto Fill-Flash

With AF-D lenses, use it for all subjects and situations.

Exposure Metering Methods With TTL Auto Fill-Flash

Camera metering method only affects ambient light: When using TTL auto fill-flash mode, the selected camera metering method affects only the ambient light measurement. The TTL flash is controlled independently in a slightly center-biased, integral manner. With an N70/F70, N90/F90, or F5 camera, a multi-sensor evaluation is performed, integrating additional distance information

Matrix metering of ambient light: Matrix metering gives optimal consideration to ambient light and subject contrast. This is the recommended metering method when using automatic flash mode. However, it is available only with AF and AF-D Nikkor lenses (except with the F4 which can also use AI/AI-S lenses).

Center-weighted metering of ambient light: In this case, ambient light is measured only in relation to middle (18%) gray, and contrast is basically not considered. This method is recommended for use with non-AF lenses or when selective control of exposure values in the center area of the image is desired (or in other areas by pre-metering and recomposing).

Spot metering of ambient light: This is recommended for metering very specific areas to establish a particular ambient-light exposure value in reference to 18% gray. F4 and F5 cameras revert to standard TTL when spot metering is used.

TTL Flash With Programmed Autoflash Camera Mode

In programmed autoflash mode, the camera selects the aperture and shutter speed automatically. The selected flash and metering method determines how the camera interacts with the SB-28.

Suitable Cameras and Flash Methods

Ideal with matrix metering: In this case, the aperture and shutter speed will be automatically selected as a function of the ambient light and subject contrast.

Suitable cameras: Programmed autoflash or TTL auto fill-flash is recommended only with N50/F50, N5005/F-401X, N6006/F-601, N8008/F-801, N70/F70, F4, F5, and N90/F90 cameras.

With AF Nikkor lenses only: Programmed autoflash is useful only with CPU lenses such as AF and AF-D Nikkor lenses.

With older cameras: Most do not have advanced autoflash mode; in standard "programmed flash," the camera is set on a fixed flash sync speed and, depending on the camera, a fixed aperture is selected.

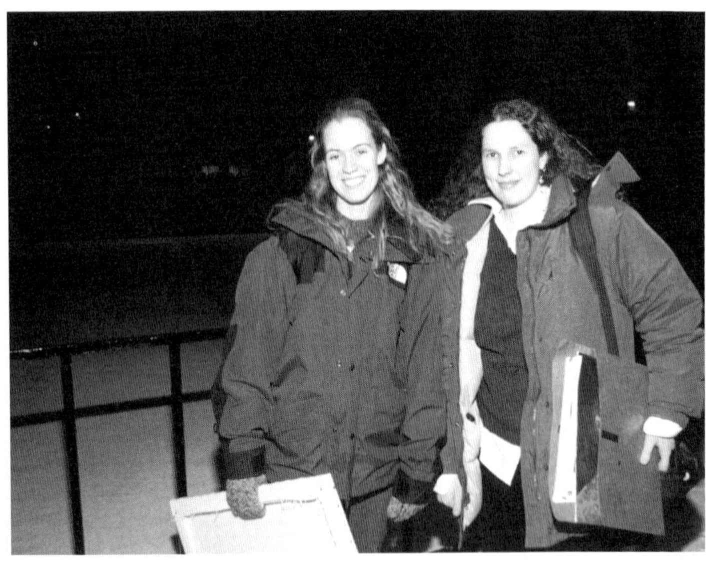

Using programmed autoflash mode, the flash illuminated the subjects, and the background remained dark.

Procedure
Simply set the camera on "P" and the metering on "matrix." See "Matrix-Balanced Automatic Fill-Flash."

When to Use TTL Flash With Programmed Autoflash
First choice: With matrix-balanced programmed flash, this method would normally be the first choice. There is hardly anything faster, and the method is highly likely to be successful.

Limits of programmed autoflash mode: If you want to select specific shutter speeds or apertures for special image effects, other exposure modes offer more flexibility. In program mode, the camera will choose aperture and shutter speed automatically, limiting the shutter speed for "Normal" flash between 1/250 and 1/60 second much of the time. The aperture will then be selected based on the sync speed. In equal lighting conditions as the ISO film speed increases, the aperture the camera may select will decrease.

Advantages of aperture priority: If you want to select specific apertures for depth of field, use auto aperture priority.

Advantages of shutter priority: If you specifically want the motion-blur effect available with slow synchronization, use shutter priority auto. The camera automatically selects an aperture to give the best possible ambient light exposure.

Advantages of manual exposure adjustment: If you want a lighter or darker background in fill-flash mode, work with manual exposure adjustment.

TTL Flash With Aperture Priority Exposure Mode

By using the camera in aperture priority camera mode "A," you can select the aperture, which allows you to control depth of field.

Suitable Cameras and Flash Methods

Older cameras: TTL flash with aperture priority automatic can be used with all Nikon cameras (except the F3) which feature TTL autoflash. This mode is also suitable for aperture priority.

Modern cameras: With cameras featuring matrix metering, aperture priority should be used primarily for artistic control.

Matrix metering with aperture priority: Only lenses with CPUs, such as AF and AF-D Nikkor lenses, are suitable (except with the F4, which also works with AI and AI-S lenses).

Procedure

- Set your camera on "A" and the SB-28 on "TTL."
- In older cameras, the shutter speed is automatically set to a fixed sync speed; in modern cameras, a sync speed is automatically selected based on ambient light conditions.
- Select the desired aperture on the lens.
- For older cameras, refer to "Standard TTL Autoflash."
- For cameras with matrix metering, refer to the section on matrix-balanced fill-flash.

When to Use TTL Flash Mode With Aperture Priority
Limits of aperture priority with TTL flash: Background brightness cannot be adapted easily to the lighter foreground with aperture priority; programmed exposure is more effective. However, the depth of field control is good.

Caution with spatially deep subjects: The aperture always affects the background brightness. An incorrect choice can result in an unnaturally light or dark background. See sections "Spatially Deep Subjects" and "Controlling Background Brightness."

TTL Flash With Shutter Priority Automatic Camera Mode

By using shutter priority automatic with TTL autoflash mode, you can select any shutter speed from the fastest available flash synchronization speed to the slowest possible shutter speed.

Suitable Cameras and Flash Methods
Older cameras: Except for the Nikon FA, older Nikon cameras do not feature shutter priority automatic.

Modern cameras: With cameras which feature shutter priority capability and matrix metering, automatic shutter priority should be used mainly for artistic purposes.

With AF and AF-D Nikkor lenses only: Only lenses with CPUs, such as AF and AF-D Nikkor lenses, allow shutter priority automatic.

Procedure

- Set your camera on "S" and the SB-28 on "TTL."
- The speed may be selected freely within the range from the highest available sync speed to the slowest possible shutter speed; the aperture is adjusted automatically.
- Otherwise, see the section on matrix-balanced TTL fill-flash.

When to Use TTL Flash With Automatic Shutter Priority
Useful for motion effects: The automatic shutter priority mode is ideal for selecting shutter speeds which will enable the

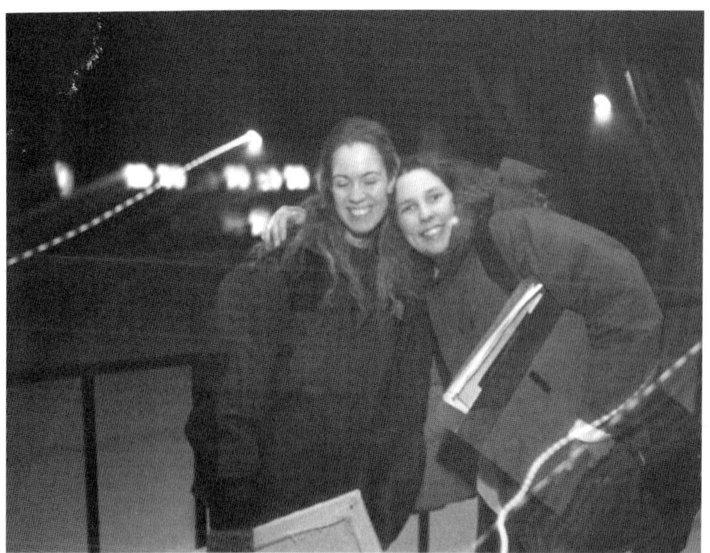

Using shutter priority automatic mode and selecting a slow shutter speed produced ambient light blur and streaks in the photo.

photographer to create blurred-motion effects. (See the section "Motion-Blur Effects.")

Risk of blur from camera shake: Camera movement causes blurred images to be superimposed on the flash image. Because this is sometimes undesirable, you must consider this result when using TTL fill-flash with the camera in shutter priority automatic mode.

Undefined depth of field: Photos of non-moving subjects are not enhanced by using shutter priority mode. Although you can change the aperture (and depth of field) by adjusting the shutter speed, it's easier to use aperture priority or manual modes, because there's no depth of field preview available in shutter priority, except on the F5, since the lens is set to the smallest aperture.

TTL Autoflash With Manual Camera Exposure Mode

By using manual adjustment, any aperture and shutter speed may be selected with TTL autoflash. The flash is controlled with TTL-metering after the shutter is released.

Suitable Cameras and Flash Methods

Older cameras: All Nikon cameras featuring TTL autoflash may be used (except the F3). They are suitable for TTL flash mode with manual exposure adjustment and center-weighted metering. If the camera automatically sets a fixed sync speed in TTL flash mode, there will essentially be no difference when compared to aperture priority.

Modern cameras: With cameras featuring matrix metering, use manual exposure adjustment primarily for artistic control.

Matrix measurement with manual exposure adjustment: Only lenses with CPUs, such as AF and AF-D Nikkor lenses, are suitable for this.

Procedure

- Set your camera on "M" and the SB-28 on "TTL."
- In older cameras, the shutter speed may be set automatically to a fixed synchronization speed.
- In modern cameras, select a speed between the fastest possible sync speed and the slowest shutter speed. (For spot and center-weighted metering, read the part of your subject where the flash exposure will be the most predominant.)
- Use the aperture ring on the lens to select the aperture.
- For older cameras, refer to "Standard TTL Autoflash."
- For cameras with matrix metering see "Matrix-Balanced Automatic Fill-Flash."

When to Use TTL Flash With Manual Exposure Mode

For specific adaptation to ambient light: In most cases, the brightness of the foreground and that of the background may be adjusted as desired.

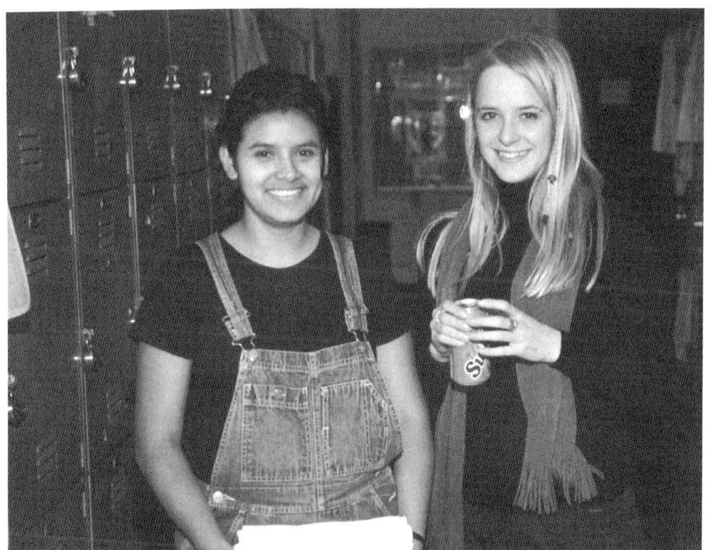

For this photo, the photographer set exposure manually to record background detail with ambient light, and the flash exposure was determined automatically with TTL autoflash.

Modern cameras: With manual exposure adjustment on modern cameras, there's no need for blind reliance on automatic fill-flash. On the other hand, some skill is required, and precious time may be spent to gain an improvement over the automatic setting.

Older cameras: With this method, you can take excellent fill-flash shots with older cameras when you make corrections affecting only the flash (film speed setting on the SB-28).

Camera and Flash Exposure Compensation in TTL Mode

Note carefully: Because the exposure of the flash may be adjusted independent of the camera exposure, a distinction must always be made between "flash exposure compensation" and "camera exposure compensation."

Exposure Compensation

Adjustments affecting the entire exposure: By changing the ISO setting or the exposure compensation dial on the camera body, the entire exposure (aperture, shutter speed *and* flash duration) will be affected in all TTL autoflash modes. This means the image foreground and background will become lighter or darker. However, care must be taken since a change in the film speed also results in a change of the guide number, and therefore the shooting range. (See *The Basics of Flash Technology.*)

Exposure compensations affecting only the flash: Flash exposure adjustments, also called "flash compensation," are made on the LCD of the flash, with the flash compensation control on the N6006/F-601, N6000/F-601m, and N70/F70, or with the MF-26 back on the N90/F90. These changes cause a variation of the flash duration, which is independent of the camera's selection of aperture and shutter speed. The foreground brightness change (from flash compensation) is different from that of the background.

Independent Manual Flash Exposure Compensation

Older cameras: Principally, cameras that do not feature automatic transfer of film-sensitivity to the SB-28 permit a different film-sensitivity setting on the flash unit than on the camera. This results in plus/minus corrections which affect only the flash.

Modern cameras: A manual flash compensation adjustment may be made instead of automatic compensation selected by fill-flash mode. Turn off auto compensation by pressing the "M" button and confirming that the person/sun or matrix-like symbol disappears from the flash display. As with automatic compensation, manual adjustment affects only the duration of the flash and not the overall exposure. The method of activation varies slightly from one camera model to the next.

N8008/F-801, N70/F70, F4, F5, and N90/F90 cameras: Adjustments may be made on the SB-28 within a range of +1 EV and -3 EV. Turn off auto compensation as stated above. Then use the plus/minus buttons to select the amount of compensation desired in 1/3-f/stop increments.

LCD using TTL auto fill-flash mode with manual flash compensation of minus 2/3 (.7) f/stop. This is possible not only with 3D matrix TTL multi-sensor automatic flash, as shown here.

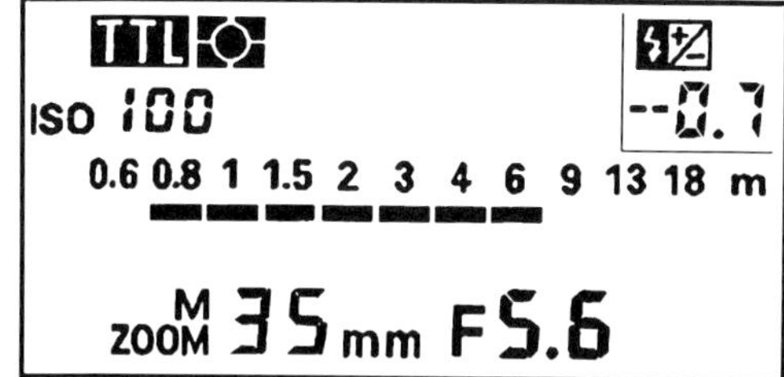

Exposure Compensation in TTL Flash Mode

For experts only: It takes a lot of knowledge and experience to produce results which are superior to the automatic flash adjustments made in auto fill-flash mode. Therefore, proceed carefully and be prepared to waste a lot of film while acquiring the expertise. I advise you to systematically, step-by-step, practice the art of advanced flash techniques by shooting many test exposures.

Limitations of Autoflash Photography

Exposure Electronics

Limitations of metering ambient light: The limits of ambient exposure metering prior to the actual flash exposure are those inherent in matrix, center-weighted or spot metering.

Limits of TTL flash: Fine adjustment of the flash's output by TTL metering during the flash exposure can have time limitations. First a small amount of time is required for the TTL metering cells to respond, electronics of the camera to evaluate, and flash unit to send the shut-off signal. Even the SB-28's switching transistor requires some time. In combination with the SB-28, the last item is probably the least restrictive; cameras are much more critical.

Film Sensitivity Range

Problem: TTL autoflash modes may be used only with film sensitivities of ISO 25 through, depending on the camera, ISO 400, or ISO 1000. If a higher film speed is used, some situations, such as close-ups, may exceed the camera's response range. If a lower film sensitivity is used, at least the close-up range will be applicable as stated. This may be tested easily by using your camera with the SB-28. (See "Slide Duplication.") It is generally recommended that you stay within the film sensitivity range of the equipment.

Film sensitivity range with exposure corrections: When exposure corrections are made (with the exposure compensation dial on the camera), which affect the entire exposure, the effect of setting a different film sensitivity (ISO) is created. This means that the range of exposure compensation values is limited to those which will not exceed the usable ISO sensitivity range. (For example, you could not make a +2 EV compensation with an ISO 25 film, the lowest sensitivity limit.) If in doubt, refer to your camera instruction manual or test this situation first with your camera.

Distance and Aperture Choices

The combination of the power output of the flash unit, film speed, and subject distance usually permit only a limited number of aperture choices for perfect operation of TTL autoflash mode. See "SB-28 Specifications" for more detailed information.

Over- and Underexposure

Risk of overexposure: This can occur even with TTL-controlled flash exposures when the distance from the subject is extremely short, as in macro or close-up photography. (See the section "Close-Up Photography With the SB-28.")

Solution: Select a smaller aperture opening in either aperture priority or manual exposure mode. Also, a neutral density filter can be attached to the front of the flash unit or the lens. In an emergency, tracing paper or standard, white typing paper may be used to reduce the flash output. An alternative is choosing a less sensitive film (lower ISO number) or setting the zoom head to a wider position, thus spreading and diffusing the light.

Risk of underexposure: This occurs when the distance to the subject is so great that the maximum amount of light emitted by the flash unit is inadequate. The maximum range of the flash, which is less with small lens apertures (high f/stop numbers) and greater with larger aperture openings (low f/stop numbers), corresponds to the range of the flash unit in "manual" mode. Even the best autoflash unit cannot deliver more than "full output."

Solution: If the power output of the flash is insufficient, move closer to the subject, use a more sensitive film (higher ISO number), or increase the aperture opening (in aperture priority or manual camera modes).

Objects or Scenes With Unusual Reflectance

Black-on-black and white-on-white: Problems may arise when flash exposures are taken of subjects that are extremely reflective or non-reflective. A bride dressed in white in front of a white wall, for example, will appear too dark in the finished photo. Or a black cat in the shade of a black car will appear too light. In these types of situations, one solution is to set the flash unit and the camera on manual flash mode. After taking a series of bracketed exposures, you should have at least one excellent shot. This can also be done in TTL, using exposure compensation to "bracket" flash duration by shifting from an assumed middle-value exposure to "overexpose" a high-reflectance subject or "underexpose" a low-reflectance subject. This has the added benefit of maintaining a single working aperture, thus consistent depth of field. The MF-26 can also be used in a similar manner in the flash bracketing mode.

The autoflash of the N70/F70, N90/F90, and F5 can handle even unusual subjects: Until now a subject exhibiting unusual reflectance could not always be handled well with automatic flash. Thanks to TTL multi-sensor control featured on the N70/F70, N90/F90, and F5 cameras with AF lenses, even "standard" flash units can cope with these subjects much better than conventional cameras. The flash exposure can be even more precise with monitor preflash offered on the SB-28 and by using type D, AF Nikkor lenses. In these situations, these cameras and the SB-28 with 3D autoflash will give "studio-quality" results.

Flash Effects With Unusual Synchronization Speeds

If your camera has the appropriate features, you can attain several interesting effects by choosing unusual synchronization speeds.

Slow Synchronization

This is a good way of taking into consideration existing light or background brightness. Slow sync can be used to lighten the background or superimpose out-of-focus moving subjects on the sharp flash image (see *Flash Methods for Special Applications*).

Older cameras: In manual camera mode, shutter speeds slower than typical flash synchronization speeds may be selected for use with any flash exposure mode (including TTL mode if available).

Modern cameras: With cameras such as the N6006/F-601, N8008/F-801, F4, F5, N70/F70, and N90/F90, manual exposure or shutter priority auto can be used to select slower shutter speeds in flash mode.

"SLOW" sync function: When flash exposures are made using the auto exposure modes "P" and "A", the N6006/F-601, N90/F90, and F5 feature an automatic adjustment of shutter speeds slower than 1/60–1/15 second, depending on the lens in use. This occurs in "SLOW" sync mode, which is set on the camera.

"REAR" sync with the second shutter curtain: With "Normal" synchronization (with the first shutter curtain) the moving subject will "push" its motion blur in front of the sharp image. This occurs because the sharp flash exposure occurred at the beginning of the movement. With second-curtain ("REAR") sync, the flash fires just before the shutter closes, causing the sharp subject to "drag" its motion blur. This corresponds with the natural way we perceive motion.

"REAR" sync on the N6006/F-601, N70/F70, N90/F90, F4, and F5: Adjustment must be set on the camera.

Older cameras: Cameras which have not been mentioned above do not have the "REAR" function.

"FP" High-Speed Flash Synchronization
With the N90/F90 and F5 only: With the SB-25, SB-26, or SB-28, these cameras permit the use of flash sync speeds up to 1/4000 second. At last, faster moving subjects can be "frozen" with fill-flash (see the section "Freezing the Action").

TTL-Controlled Multiflash Mode

Suitable Cameras and Flash Units

Principle: The camera, main flash unit, and auxiliary flash units are connected with each other using TTL cords and adapters. All flash units are TTL-controlled by the camera. With a little experience, backgrounds can be lightened, intriguing backlit exposures simulated, and much more. Thanks to TTL autoflash, extremely poor exposures are almost impossible.

Suitable cameras: With the SB-28 (or SB-25 or SB-26), all Nikon cameras with TTL autoflash (except the F3) allow the simultaneous control of several TTL flash units.

Suitable flash units: Only original Nikon TTL system flash units (see the operating instructions of each unit) should be used for multiple flash exposures.

Combining flash units from other manufacturers is not recommended: When other brand flash units are used, not only is it possible that errors may result, but also your camera and flash units may be damaged! Nikon-compatible flash units from another manufacturer should be used only if this manufacturer assures that these concerns are unwarranted.

Accessories for TTL Multiflash

Relatively few accessories are required. In addition to the flash units themselves, you need one or more distribution units (TTL multiflash adapter AS-10), a remote cord (TTL remote cord SC-17), and a few connecting cords (TTL multiflash sync cords SC-18 or SC-19). If you mount the SB-26 or SB-28 directly on the camera, you do not need the SC-17 because they have a built-in TTL multiflash terminal. On the other hand, an SC-17 cord is always handy to have for taking off-camera flash pictures or when using a flash bracket such as a Stroboframe bracket.

Recommendations for Using TTL Multiflash Mode

Number of flash units which can be combined: To prevent overloading the camera's electronics, use a limited number of flash units. To assist in determining the correct combination of units, Nikon systems flash units are assigned a "power coefficient number." As examples, the power coefficient of the SB-20 is (9), SB-22 (6), SB-23 (4), SB-24 (1), SB-25 (1), SB-26 (1), SB-27 (1), and SB-28 (1). The number of flash units connected with each other should not exceed a power coefficient total of 20. This means, for example, that you may connect 20 SB-28s, one SB-28 + three SB-20s, or one SB-28 + four SB-23s, or one SB-28 + one SB-20 + one SB-22 + one SB-23 unit. Generally, it is not recommended that you use more than five flash units regardless of the coefficient total. This is because more than five units pointed at the same subject may cause an increase in exposure from normal. (Residual exposure accumulates as flash duration is controlled [the light output is not OFF instantly].) If you must use more than five flash units, don't go over the power coefficient total of 20. And don't point the flash units all at the same area. Make test exposures first to determine any necessary exposure compensation.

Overload: If too many flash units are connected with each other, the camera and/or flash units may not fire. To "reset," the main flash unit must be switched off and removed from the camera. Then each flash unit should be switched on and off at least once. Of course, if necessary, use fewer units. Recheck the combination by referring to the coefficient numbers above.

TTL Flash With Non-TTL Slave

Principle: A TTL master flash unit, camera-mounted or used off-camera with a cable, triggers several remote (slave) flash units. These slave units are triggered in manual mode or by a dedicated "computer control" which is independent of the camera. Correctly exposed photos are obtained when the slave flash settings are adjusted to exactly match those of the camera aperture, film speed, and *its* own distance relative to the subject.

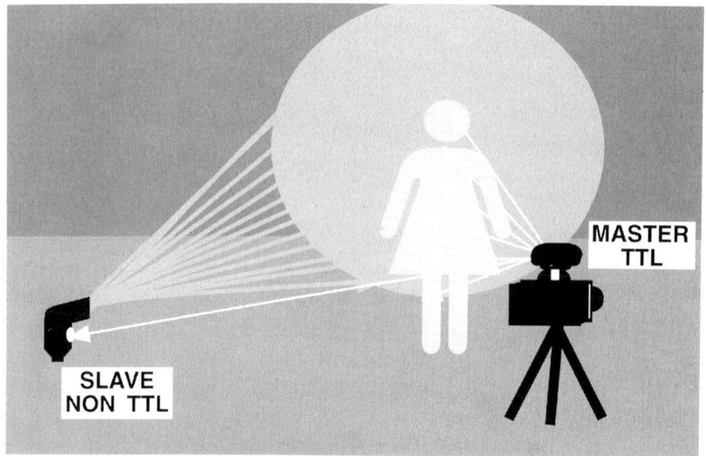

Typical slave flash situation: The SB-26 acts as non-TTL slave for basic lighting of the main subject and background. The on-camera master flash determines the TTL-controlled brightness of the main subject.

Advantage: Compared with TTL multiflash, there is no confusion caused by too many cables, and the flash results can be just as good. It does not matter whether a TTL or slave method is used: Ultimately, either multiflash method requires careful matching of output and spatial distribution of all TTL flash units involved. Incidentally, this also applies to wireless TTL flash control as offered by other manufacturers (Minolta, Metz). (To be better, the TTL control of the camera's computer would have to know the position and power of each individual flash unit and—in flash mode—switch off each individual unit. Sadly, it doesn't do this.)

SB-28 Without Integrated Slave Function

Unlike the SB-26, the SB-28 was not designed with a wireless remote feature. The SB-28 may be operated off-camera when connected to a remote flash trigger; Nikon offers such a wireless remote flash controller, the SU-4. This small (2.5 x 2.1 x 1.1-inch or 6.3 x 5.3 x 2.8-cm) accessory uses an infrared beam to trigger one, two, or more off-camera accessory flash units. One flash unit must be connected to the camera, and each off-camera accessory flash unit is mounted in the hot shoe of an SU-4. When the on-camera flash fires, an infrared beam triggers the SU-4 to fire the remote

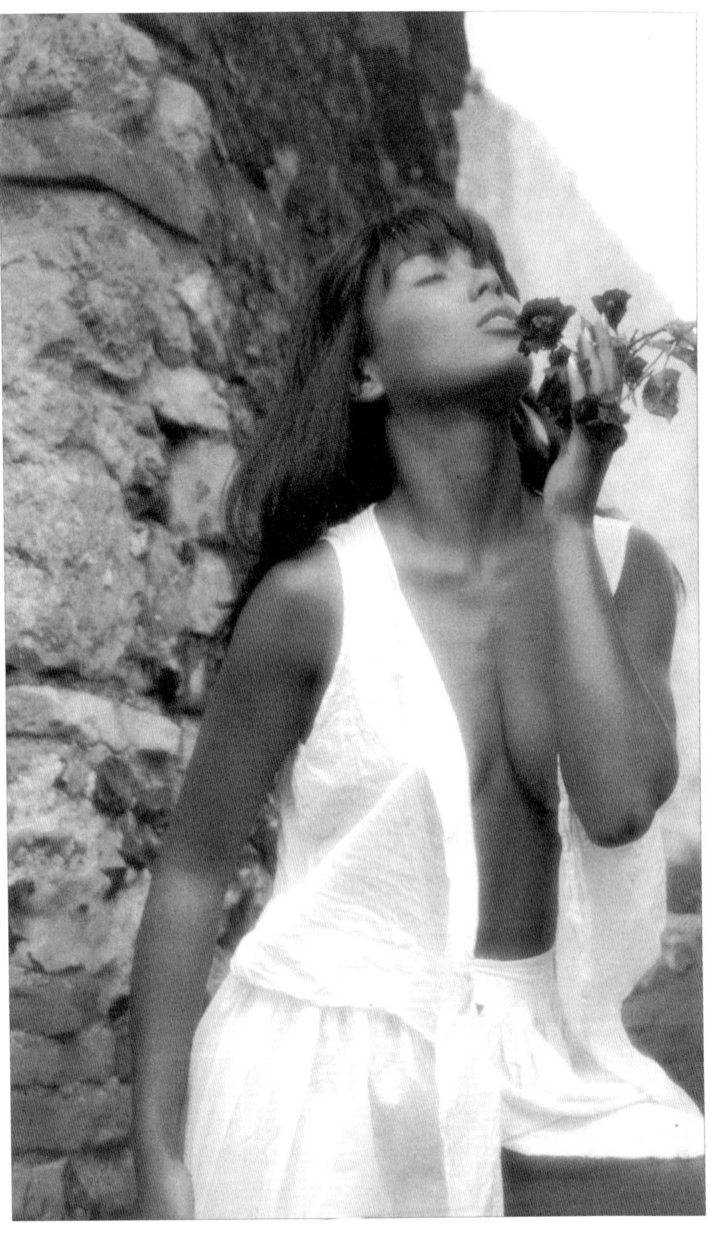

units. Audible beeps emitted by the SU-4 signal correct or incorrect exposure. The number of remote flash units and their positions determine the lighting effect. The SU-4 can be used with Nikon speedlights in multiple-flash lighting setups to reduce background shadow. It can also be used with speedlights acting as second lights for fill- or main-light purposes. The SU-4 maintains TTL flash control at distances up to 23 feet (7 meters). In manual flash mode, it offers a range of up to 131 feet (40 meters).

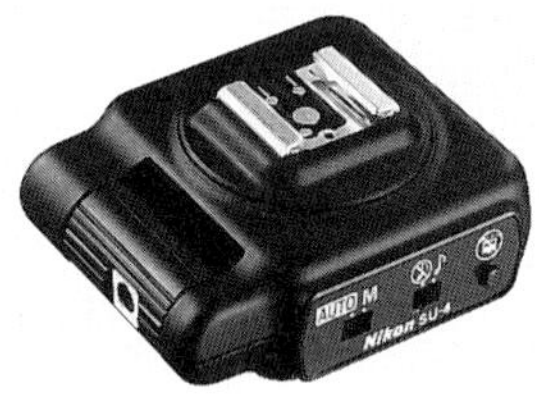

Wireless Remote Flash Controller SU-4

< Softening the effect of the flash with a diffuser card and a "grainy" soft-focus filter resulted in this pleasing photograph. Photograph: Bob Shell

SB-26 With Integrated, Adjustable Slave-Flash Sensor

The SB-26 features an integrated slave-flash sensor and is an extremely powerful remote flash system compatible with all cameras and flash units belonging to the Nikon family of products.

The SB-26, however, distinguishes itself from other slave-flash systems because it permits additional fine-tuning. If the slave-flash selector switch is set on "S," the SB-26 used as slave is triggered "simultaneously" with the TTL master flash. If the setting is "D," the SB-26 is triggered with a "delay." With all cameras, the setting "D" causes the flash exposure to be affected predominantly by the TTL master flash. N70/F70, N90/F90, and F5 cameras should be used only with "D" because the highly sensitive multi-sensor TTL flash control of these cameras may be impaired by simultaneously triggered slave flashes. (Different from conventional TTL controls, the flash control of these cameras will compute the entire flash exposure time again from the time the flash is triggered, based on the *first* reflected portion of flash light. As a result, the entering diffuse slave flash light would cause underexposure through the TTL master flash.)

Procedure

- Use a standard on-camera flash unit as the *master* flash unit in TTL mode.
- Use this TTL main flash in such a manner that your subject would be exposed correctly by this flash alone, if necessary.
- Select the spatial location, light output setting, and flash angle on the SB-26 *slave* unit in such a manner that this flash provides the "basic brightness" of the overall subject (or background fill-flash), if necessary.
- Remember that the film speed must be set manually on the SB-26.
- With N70/F70, N90/F90, and F5 cameras, set the slave flash switch on the SB-26 on "D." With other cameras, set it on "S." (If "D," see the Nikon manual.)
- As a rule, now select the same or a slightly smaller aperture on the camera (autoflash mode or TTL auto fill-flash), which would be required for exposures with the SB-26 slave alone.
- When the flash is triggered, the flash exposure is TTL-adjusted precisely on the main subject, whereas the slave unit acts as fill-flash for the remainder of the scene.

Flash Methods for Special Applications

Flash Exposures in Low Light or Darkness

"Black Holes" in Deep Subjects
Problem: Since the light released by the flash decreases in proportion to the square of the distance, a distinct distance between the foreground and the background frequently becomes a "black hole."

Flash exposures with slow shutter speeds: The "black hole" situation occurs typically in larger, poorly-illuminated rooms. If there is noticeable ambient light and the subjects are not moving, this situation can be handled by using a slower shutter speed. Unlike the choice of aperture, which affects the flash-exposed foreground, the choice of shutter speed affects only the ambient light (and therefore the background) exposure.

For almost all cameras: By using manual exposure adjustment on the camera, shutter speeds slower than the typical flash synchronization speed may be selected for use with flash (even with TTL flash mode).

"SLOW" sync: When an aperture appropriate for the desired depth of field has been selected on the camera, this flash mode with matrix metering will automatically adjust the background brightness in accordance with the exposure time, in aperture priority and programmed exposure. Don't forget to use a tripod and a self-timer or cable release to prevent camera movement.

"SLOW" sync for moving subjects: Moving subjects will be blurred with low ambient light and slow shutter speeds. If this is desirable, it is better to use "SLOW" mode with automatic aperture adjustment.

Multiple Flash Studio-Type Lighting of Spatially Deep Subjects
Use of several flash units: To lighten the background, you can use several flash units, in addition to the camera-mounted flash, either with TTL cords or with flash slaves. However, because TTL auto fill-flash responds to the ambient light metered before the flash is fired, additional flash units may over-lighten the background. Therefore, a fully manual flash exposure determined by using a hand-held flash meter is recommended. (See "Studio Flash Photography.")

Backlighting With High Contrast and Strong Ambient Light

Balanced Exposure of Background and Foreground
Problem: When backlighting is balanced with flash, the object is for the foreground and background to exhibit similar brightness levels. With conventional TTL autoflash, this is possible only through specific compensation of the background exposure. And without corresponding flash compensation, the foreground could possibly appear too light. Additional information and appropriate methods are described in the chapter *Flash Methods and Applications*. Below is a brief overview of the important control features available on modern cameras with matrix-balanced TTL fill-in autoflash.

Programmed autoflash is best: Whenever a noticeable amount of ambient light is present, for example, in the case of backlit exposures, an appropriate combination of aperture and shutter speed will balance the foreground and the background. The simplest fully automatic method is provided by the combination of matrix metering, program, and TTL automatic fill-flash.

Backlighting alternative–manual exposure adjustment: Manual exposure with spot or center-weighted metering of the background provides similarly good or even better results with TTL automatic fill-flash. Note that F5 and F4 cameras perform standard TTL when set to spot metering.

Controlling Background Brightness

Problem: It's not always desirable that the background and the foreground have the same brightness level resulting from fill-flash. To "set-off" the main subject against the background, consider making the background darker or lighter. Practically all recent Nikon cameras offer this option using manual exposure adjustment in combination with TTL autoflash.

Procedure

- The SB-28 must be set on "TTL" and *not* on "M."
- Using manual camera exposure mode, first set the aperture appropriate for a shutter speed between 1/60 and 1/250 second. Meter the main subject by using either spot or center-weighted metering and then adjust the exposure as if shooting without flash.
- The aperture determined in this manner may be closed down approximately 2 to 3 stops to make the background distinctly darker or opened up approximately 2 to 3 stops to make the background distinctly lighter.
- After some trial and error, you should be able to achieve the desired effect on the first try.

Slower shutter speeds are not useful for compensation: In manual exposure mode, shutter speeds of less than 1/60 second are not very helpful for exposure compensation of backlit subjects. Slow shutter speeds for exposures with little available light, however, will produce motion blurs.

Additional Adjustment of Background and Foreground Brightness

By using opposing exposure compensations on the camera and SB-28, the brightness values of the foreground and background may be brought closer to each other. However, to arrive at reliable results, make a few test exposures first.

White or black main subject: These exposures were taken with the N90/F90 and an AF-D Nikkor lens in 3D-TTL multi-sensor auto fill-flash mode. Without exposure compensation, the white subject appears too gray. Depending on the desired brightness, an aperture adjustment of approximately +1.3 to +2 f/stops should be made. The black subject is even trickier because it is highly reflective. The 3D autoflash feature actually handles this quite well; with zero adjustment, the black gloves are only a bit too gray and appear quite natural with -0.7 compensation. Depending on the desired rendition, a less shiny subject could tolerate a somewhat greater minus correction. Conventional TTL autoflash would require even more significant compensation. ➢

"Freezing" motion with high-speed sync "FP": High-speed synchronization permits flash exposures with extremely short shutter speeds of up to 1/4000 second. (A) was exposed at f/4 at 1/60 second without flash. As you can see, the movement was blurred. (B) was exposed at f/4 and synchronized normally at 1/60 second. TTL fill-flash was used, and an out-of-focus ambient light image was superimposed on the sharp flash image. (C) was exposed manually at f/5.6 with FP synchronization for 1/2000 second; there are still a few visible traces of movement. (D) was exposed at f/4 with FP-synchronization at 1/4000 second This has "frozen" the motion completely. ➢➢

Effect of total exposure compensation in TTL flash mode: This series of exposures was taken in matrix-balanced programmed TTL auto fill-flash with aperture adjustments of +1.5, +0.7, 0.0, and -1.5 (E, F, G, and H). Because aperture changes affect the exposure of both ambient light and flash, the brightness of the foreground and background were uniformly changed.

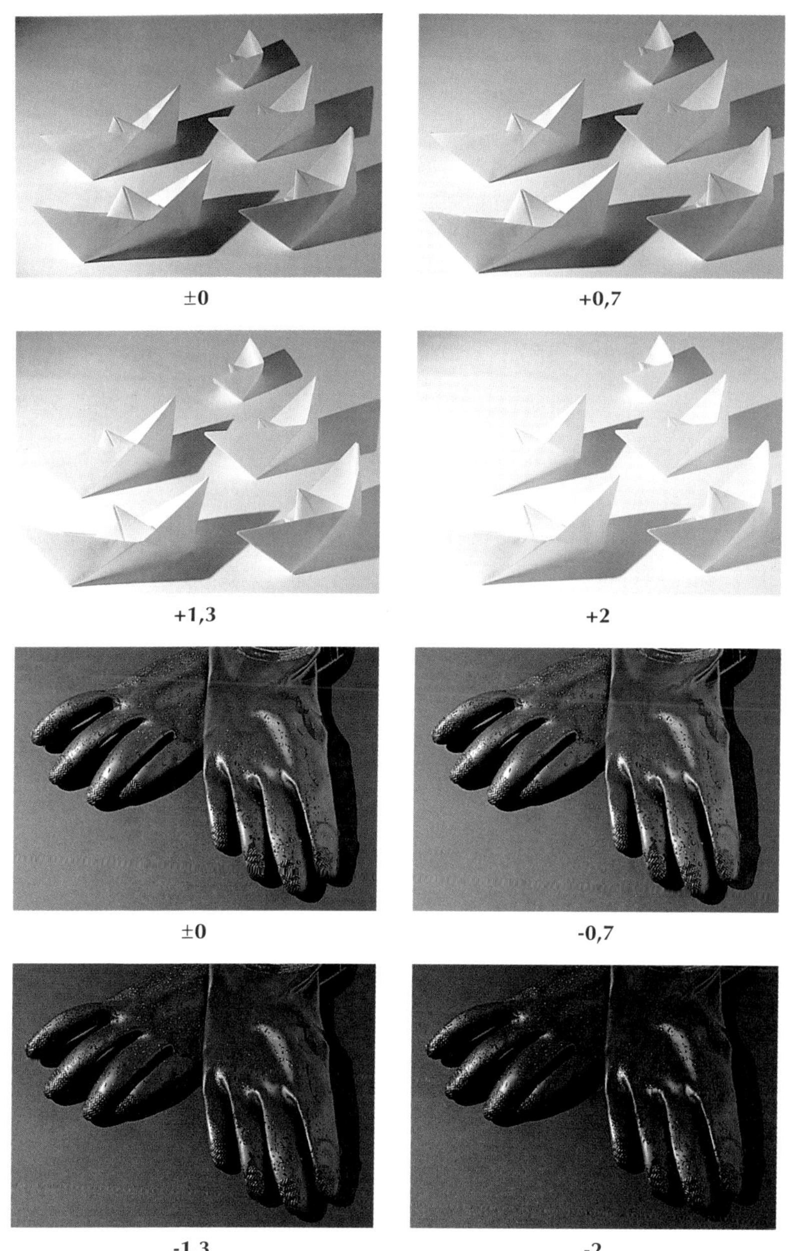
±0
+0,7
+1,3
+2
±0
-0,7
-1,3
-2

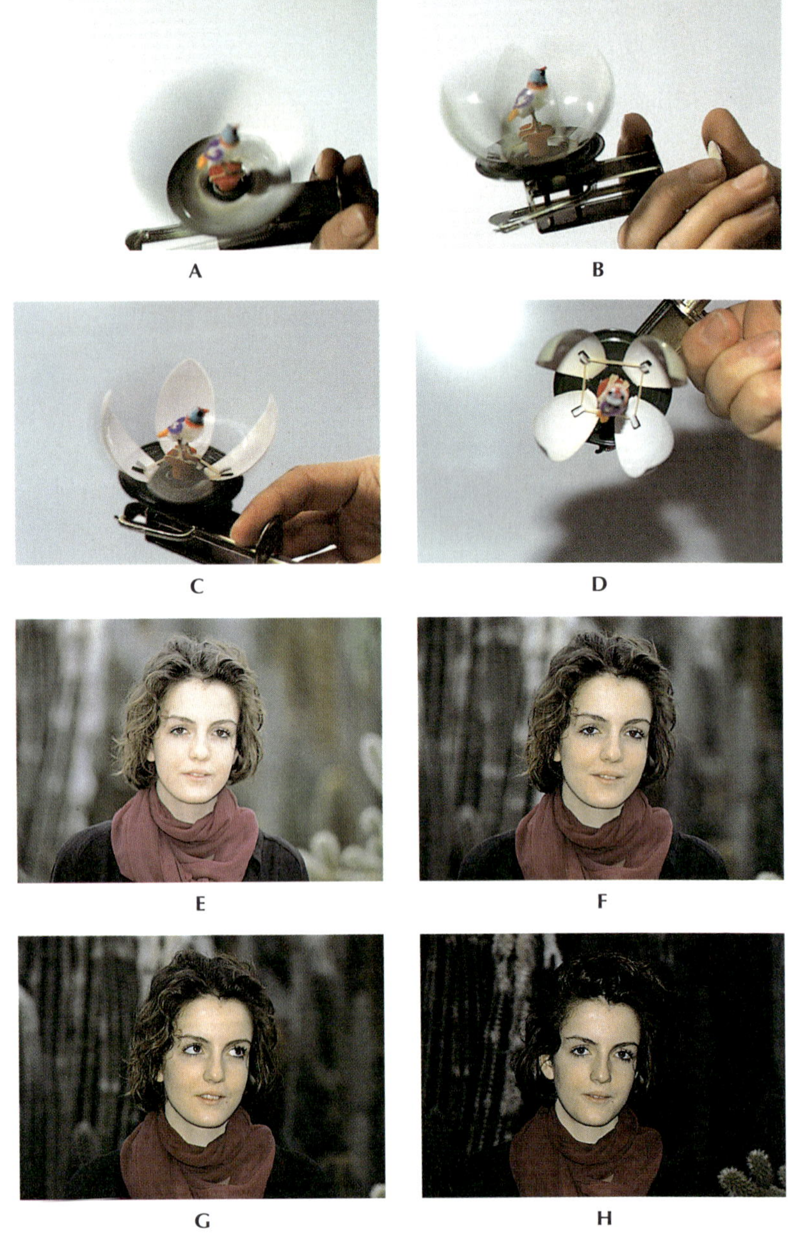

A

B

C

D

E

F

G

H

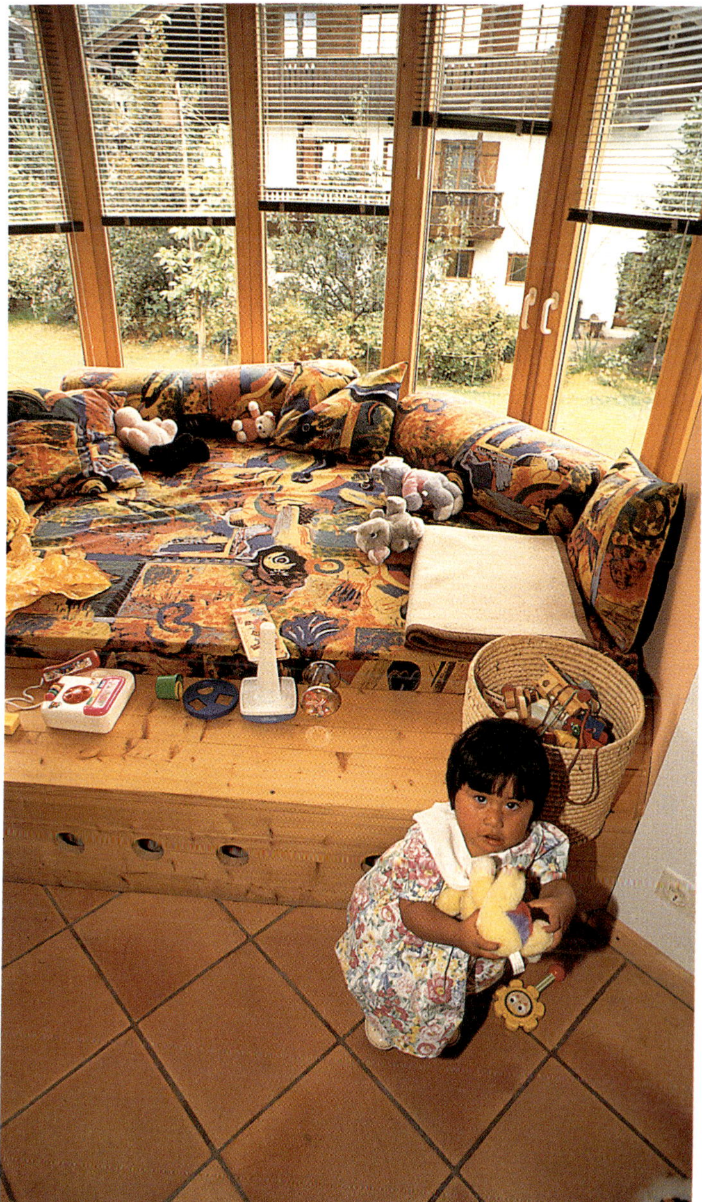

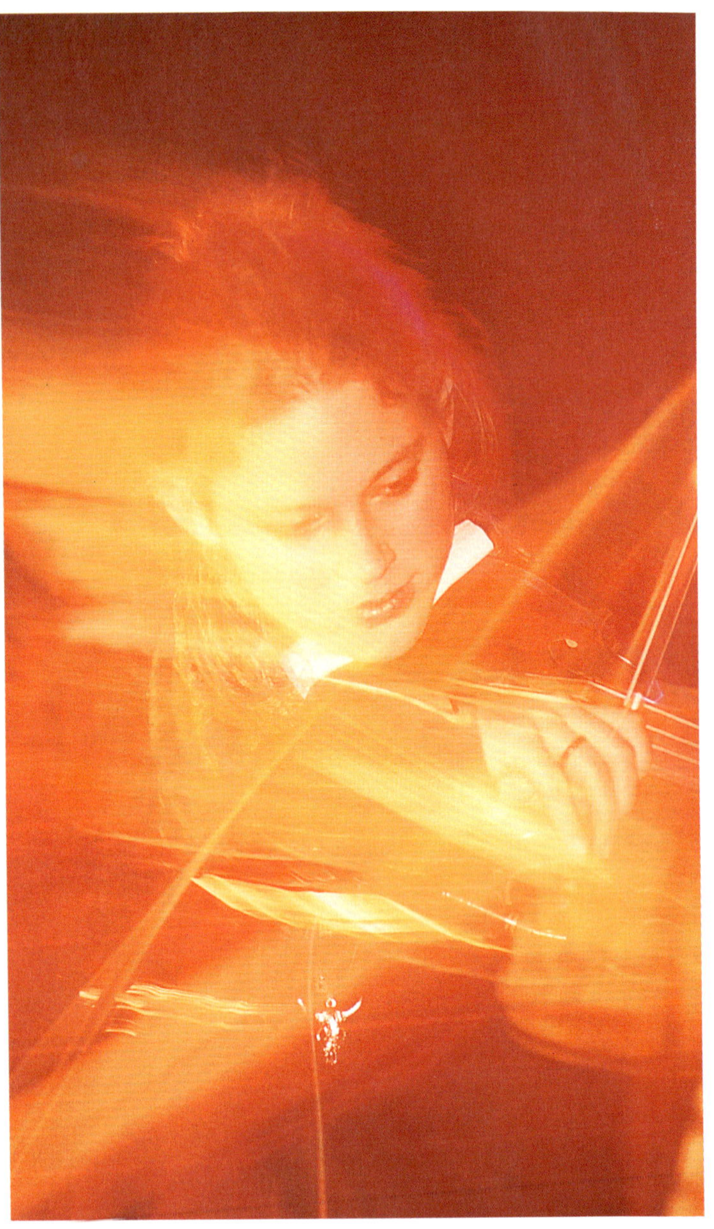

Artistic Control of Depth of Field

Aperture affects depth of field and background brightness: You may use TTL fill-flash with aperture priority or manual exposure to select an aperture appropriate for the desired sharpness of the background. However, this is possible only when the background is relatively close to the main subject (the distance between the camera and subject is twice as far as the distance between the subject and background). If the distance to the background is too great, light falloff will be noticeable and a change in aperture will affect both the depth of field and the brightness of the background.

Great depth of field with slight light decrease and strong ambient light: If depth of field is important to you, select a small aperture so that the main subject and background will be in focus. Due to TTL flash control, both the subject and background will appear similar in brightness.

Shallow depth of field with slight light decrease and average ambient light: Use a large aperture if a very short depth of field range is desired and the main subject is to be setoff against an out-of-focus background of similar brightness.

Great depth of field with substantial light decrease and little ambient light: First select an aperture appropriate for the depth of field desired. Then combine it with the above "adjustment of a light or dark background" method by adjusting the exposure time. A flower in a relatively dark forest would be setoff against the dark background because the great depth of field requires a the small

Fully automatic fill-flash power: With a 20mm Nikkor lens and programmed auto-exposure in matrix-controlled TTL multi-sensor flash mode, this shot was perfect at first try without requiring additional corrections.

Flash pictures with motion traces: This passionate violinist was shot with a 180mm AF-D Nikkor lens, an autoflash setting of f/5.6 and "SLOW" flash sync at 1/8 second. This makes her motions beautifully visible.

aperture and, generally, a shutter speed of 1/60 to 1/250 second. However, slower shutter speeds would create a lighter background. This method is suitable only for non-moving subjects. Use a tripod and a cable release or a self-timer to prevent blurred images.

Normally Bright, Out-of-Focus Backgrounds

Problem: A large aperture is required where you want the subject "separated" from a rather bright, out-of-focus background. However, normally short flash sync speeds up to 1/250 second can result in unnaturally bright backgrounds, depending on the ambient light conditions.

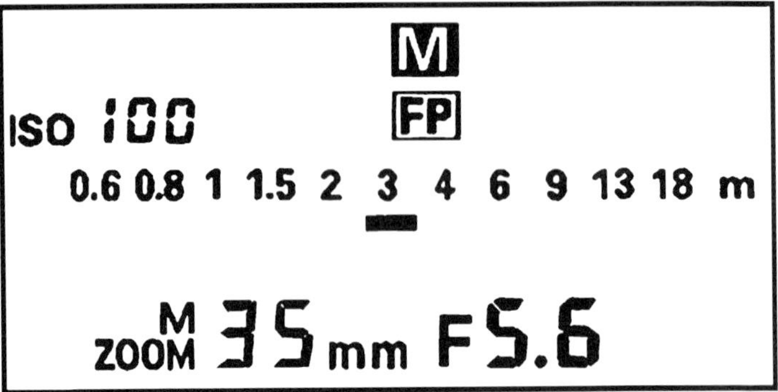

LCD showing the "FP" flash mode.

High-speed synchronization "FP": Faster sync speeds of up to 1/4000 second are possible when the function "FP" is used on the N90/F90, F5 cameras and the SB-25, SB-26, or SB-28.

Procedure

- Set the camera on manual exposure and the SB-28 flash unit on "M" and use the plus/minus buttons to select "FP."
- Then set the aperture for the desired depth of field. The distance to the main subject may be varied by changing the zoom-head setting as indicated on the LCD.
- Finally, adjust the background exposure by selecting a shutter speed of up to 1/4000 second, using spot or center-weighted metering.

- The N90/F90 camera and the SB-28 must operate without TTL control when set on "FP." Therefore, when the aperture has been selected, the distance to the main subject displayed on the flash unit must be maintained *exactly*.

Motion-Blur Effects

Superimposing Flash and Ambient Light Images

Objective: Even when using flash, you can create motion blurs intentionally. The flash image is superimposed over a second, blurred, existing-light image exposed at a slow shutter speed. This can produce very interesting motion-blur images.

Creating motion blurs: For example, let's use a shutter-speed setting of 1/8 second. During the flash exposure (approximately 1/1000 second), the subject is frozen by the short duration of the flash. However, the subject is also illuminated additionally by normal ambient light during the entire 1/8-second exposure. With a moving subject, its sharp flash image will be superimposed with a second, out-of-focus ambient-light image. Also, if the shutter speed is slow, you can intentionally cause the blur by moving the camera. Undoubtedly, this can be an interesting field for experimentation.

Procedure

- Set your camera on shutter priority or manual exposure mode.
- Switch the SB-28 to "TTL" (optionally with fill-flash or matrix function).
- Select a slower shutter speed appropriate for the desired motion effect.

Note: Depending on the camera model, you can attain similar effects with weak ambient light when using programmed exposure or aperture priority and "SLOW" sync.

Natural motion blurs with "REAR": When using slow shutter speeds, F5, N70/F70, N90/F90, F5, and N6006/F-601 cameras can be switched to "REAR" flash mode. "REAR" signifies synchronization with the second shutter curtain. In practice, this means that the ambient light exposure occurs before the release of the flash. This effect is obvious only with slow shutter speeds, noticeable ambient light, and moving objects. With conventional synchronization, the object "pushes" its motion blur unnaturally in front of itself. The second shutter curtain sync causes the object to "drag" the blur behind itself. Certainly the most suitable mode for slow shutter speeds is shutter priority, or manual exposure adjustment. Incidentally, this situation often requires some testing before you can obtain the best results.

Freezing the Action

Problem: In the past, the shutter speed range of most cameras included 1/1000 second as the fastest exposure time for non-blurred representation of fast action. With fast speeds up to 1/4000 and 1/8000 second now offered by modern Nikon cameras, normal daylight may not be adequate for high-quality action photography. Therefore, flash photography is an important method of producing good exposures.

Very Low Ambient Light With "B"
With TTL control: The camera is set to the desired aperture and the shutter speed set to "B" or "bulb" in manual camera exposure mode. (Use manual focus on AF cameras.) When a flash exposure is taken in very low ambient light, or even in complete darkness in TTL mode, the moving object is recorded only during the relatively short duration of the flash. Depending on the reflectance of the object, improperly exposed images may result.

Fully manual control: This requires total darkness. (Use manual focus on AF cameras.) The camera shutter is opened for a given period of time in "B" mode by holding down the shutter release or using a locking cable release. The SB-28, set on "M," is triggered via the test flash button. Then the shutter is closed. The distance from the (preferably off-camera) flash unit to the subject must match the selected aperture. If possible, a series of bracketed exposures should be made by increasing and decreasing the aperture setting or decreasing the manual power ratios– 1/1, 1/2, 1/4, 1/8, 1/16, 1/32, 1/64.

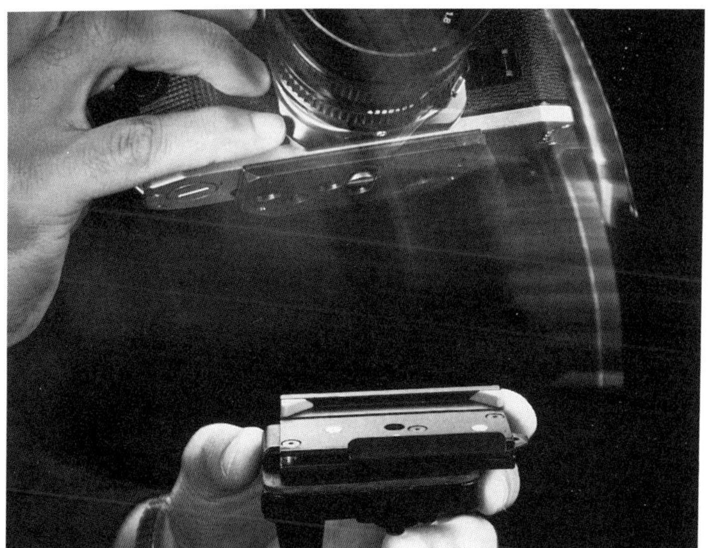

This product shot of the Stroboframe Camera Auto Quick Release is an example of effective use of motion blur.

Reducing the Flash Duration a Minimum of 1/8700 Second By Varying the Output

By reducing the manual flash output level in combination with a "B" exposure (see previous text), flash exposures may be taken in total darkness with specific duration (see "SB-28 Specifications").

Ample Ambient Light and High-Speed Synchronization "FP"

Problem: If there is an abundance of ambient light and you make a fill-flash exposure of a moving subject, normal flash synchronization times will not be useful. Even at 1/250 second, the sharp flash image is usually superimposed with a blurred, out-of-focus, ambient-light image. The only solution is to use high-speed synchronization "FP" (currently only with the SB-25, SB-26, or SB-28 and N90/F90 or F5).

Procedure

- Set the camera on manual exposure mode and the SB-28 flash unit on main switch position "M." Use the plus/minus buttons to select "FP."

- To freeze motion, select a shutter speed of up to 1/4000 second is on the camera along with an aperture appropriate for the required depth of field.
- Because the N90/F90 and F5, plus the flash unit set on "FP," all operate without TTL control, you must maintain the *exact* distance from the main subject recommended on the flash unit.
- You can change the distance via the aperture and the lens focal length.

Creating Motion Sequences

Stroboscopic (Repeating) Flash Mode

Problem: To create a motion-study sequence, the image must be broken down into several sharply focused, partial images.

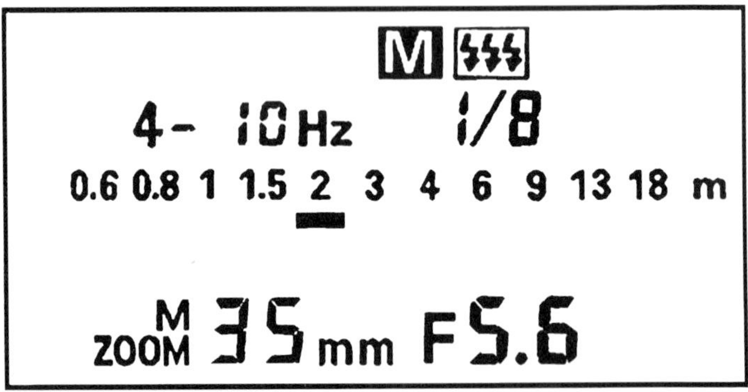

LCD using stroboscopic flash mode.

Operation: The SB-28's stroboscopic function allows the firing of a sequence of several very short flashes during a normal to longer flash synchronization period. In sports and science, stroboscopic exposures permit the analysis of rapid motion. The SB-28 makes this effect possible when used with any camera having a hot shoe.

Procedure

- Set the camera on manual exposure mode and select a shutter speed (if it can be varied during flash mode) appropriate for the subject.

- Slow shutter speeds (as slow as possible) and even "B" may be selected in total darkness. In this case, an out-of-focus "ghost image" caused by continuous light will not occur.
- Set the flash unit's main selection switch on stroboscopic mode ("M" + multiple flash symbol).
- Now use the "SEL" and plus/minus buttons to set the flash frequency* (the number of flashes fired per second) between 1 and 50 Hz ...
- ... then the number of flashes per frame* (1 through 90) ...
- ... then the flash output* between 1/8 and 1/64.
- Focus on your subject (manual focus is best with AF cameras).
- The flash unit's LCD will display the aperture appropriate for the distance, which should be set on the lens.
- Select the shutter speed so that:

shutter speed = flashes per frame ÷ flash frequency

Flashes per frame: This depends on the flash output and the flash frequency. For example, with a flash output of 1/16 and a flash frequency of 7 Hz, you can pre-set a sequence of 20 flashes per frame. With 1/64, you can pre-set a sequence of 44 flashes.

Shutter speed: In total darkness, "B" is a good solution. Otherwise, use the above formula. If more flashes per frame are entered than are appropriate for the selected flash frequency and exposure time, additional flashes are fired without effect.

Darkness and matching background: This formula is a good starting point if the subject is moving against a dark background with no overlapping exposures. If the flash bursts overlap, causing cumulative exposure in some areas, stop down the aperture or increase the flash-to-subject distance. Keep in mind that exposure recommendations are based on optimal conditions. For best results, first make some test exposures.

Studio Flash Photography

Why in the Studio and Not on Location?

Studio photography enables the photographer to totally control

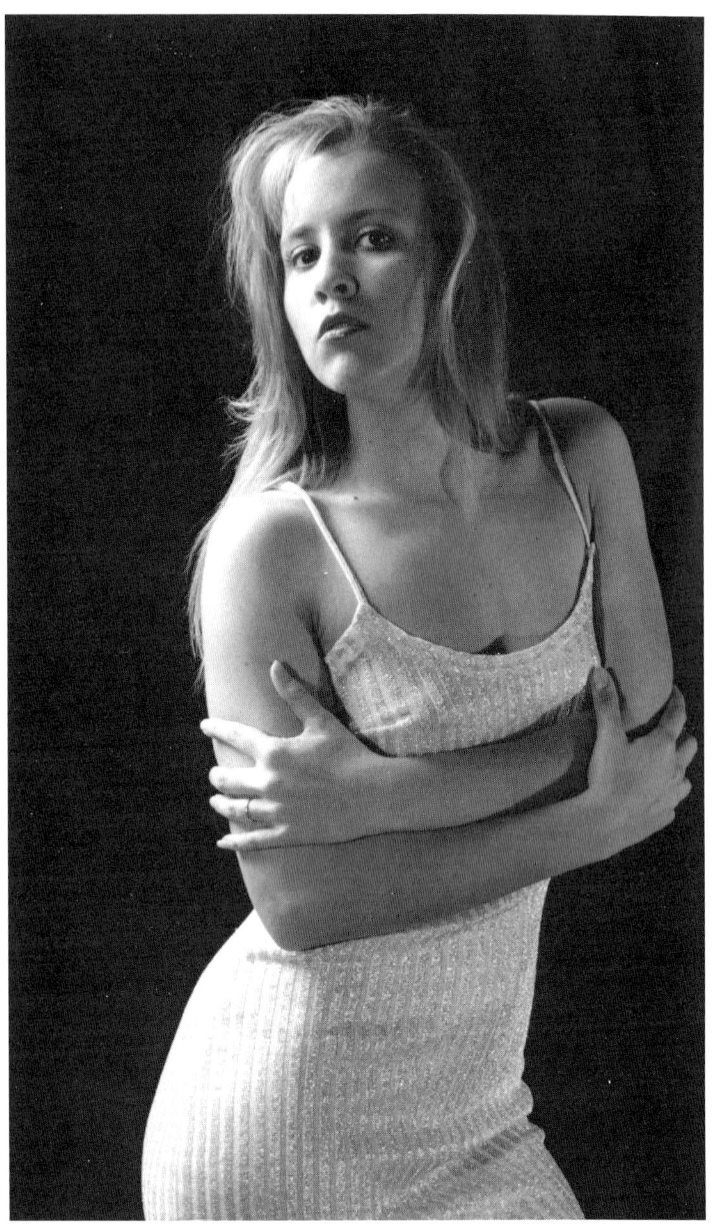

the lighting conditions. Also weather is never an obstacle. Flash pictures taken in the studio can meet the precise lighting specifications envisioned by the photographer and the client. In practice, this means that a distinction in ambient light and flash light, or in a foreground lightened by a flash and a background illuminated by existing light (such as with TTL fill-flash) would be pointless in the studio.

Composing With Light

Number, intensity, and position of studio flash units: A specific light composition is attained by using several high-power studio flash units and appropriate generators. Studio-type flash photography allows the use of the most varied reflectors and luminescent surfaces (for example, bright spot-lights or soft, hazy-lights) and the simulation of all types of light and lighting angles ranging from bright sunlight to the soft light of a northern window. This is possible with a light output which, if desired, permits even small apertures with the use of low-sensitivity films. Because the flash duration of most studio flash units is approximately 1/300 second or less, normal human movements are frozen and, if desired, hand-held shooting is possible.

Reflectors and diffusers: You can use reflectors and diffusers (diffusing screens placed between the flash lamp and subject) in the studio to further modify the light output.

Modeling lights: To evaluate the lighting effect, studio flash units have a built-in halogen modeling light, which varies its intensity to match the selected flash output. This enables the photographer to make a reasonably realistic evaluation of the lighting effect on the subject. This is an advantage over camera-mounted flash units, such as the SB-28, which leave one literally, "shooting in the dark." It is obvious that an automatic flash unit would not perform adequately in such a finely-tuned flash illumination setup. Finally, each studio flash lamp can be assigned a different lighting effect.

It doesn't take a lot of professional lighting equipment to produce a dramatic portrait in the studio. Photograph: Bob Shell

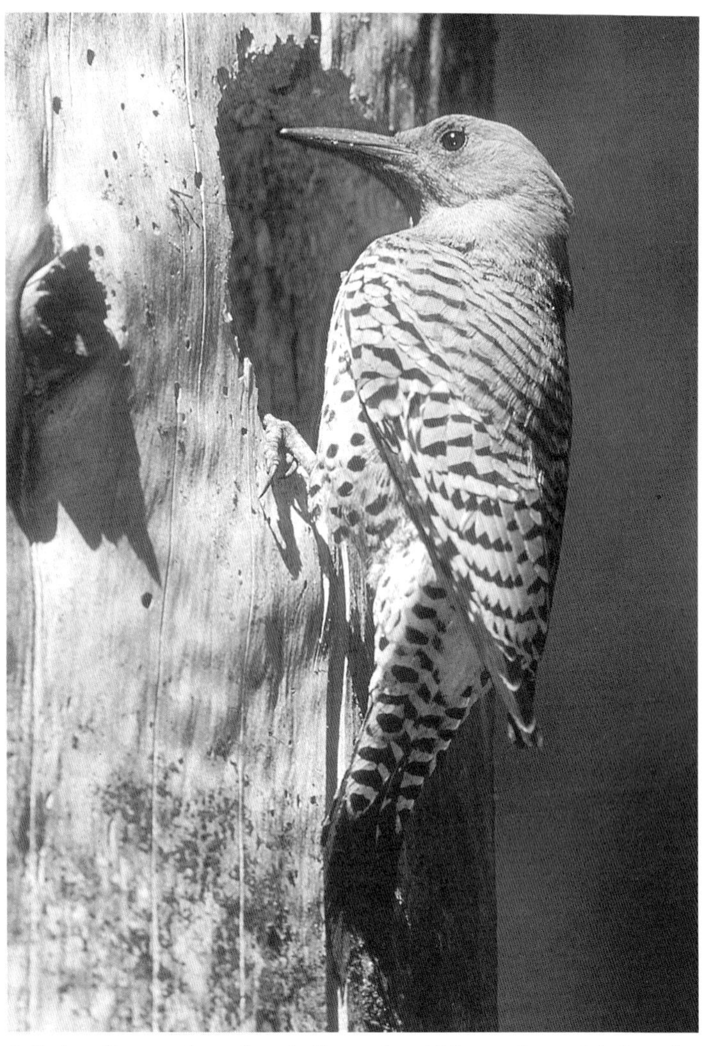

A flash unit was set up close to the nest and triggered remotely in order to get this photograph.

Camera-controlled flash cannot detect this situation. (Ideally, a properly functioning studio flash computer would be able to do this. And rumor has it that a number of studio flash manufacturers are busily working on this.)

Manual Flash Exposure Metering

After all of the values have been set on the flash units and generators, determine the camera's aperture by firing test flashes. To do this, use a flash meter, pointing it at the subject to measure the total brightness reflecting from the subject. Or, while standing at the subject's position, point the meter in the direction of the camera to measure incident light (the total light falling on the subject). Assuming the subject has normal reflectance characteristics, the two meter readings should be about the same. With either method of measurement, you now have the total of all direct and indirect light hitting the subject at the time of exposure. Provided you set the correct film sensitivity on the meter, you can read the correct aperture off it and set the camera's lens accordingly.

Flash Triggering

Cable: Studio flash set-ups can be triggered via a flash cable, which is plugged into the camera's flash sync terminal. (If this is not present on your camera, use a commercially available flash-shoe adapter.)

Remote Triggering: Another option might be to use a hot-shoe-mounted flash unit (SB-28) and fire it indirectly at the ceiling, for example, to trigger the studio flash system. Most studio flash systems include photo cells (slave units), which will simultaneously trigger other units. Another more advanced method of cordless flash triggering is the use of infrared-triggering devices. These are superior to visible light triggers because they are unaffected by stray light from other sources. The Wein company makes several infrared flash triggering systems that enable you to trigger multiple units at the same time. The unit attached to the camera triggers all other Wein units simultaneously. Multi-channel units even allow you to selectively trigger certain flashes independently of the others. This is by far the most elegant solution in any studio-type flash situation. For further information, contact the Wein division of the Tiffen Company (address on page 4).

Getting the Best Results With Any Subject

You can successfully photograph just about any subject with the SB-28. Obviously, one SB-28 will not illuminate the nave of a cathedral, a market square at night, or a gymnasium. However, the SB-28's power output will be more than adequate for most common subjects or situations.

Nudes

Lens recommendation: In general, the ideal focal lengths for portraits are approximately 80mm to 105mm. Full-length close-ups of nudes may, however, require a wide-angle lens. In this case, care must be taken that perspective distortions inherent with wide-angle lenses will enhance, rather than degrade, the total image.

Soft, diffused illumination: When photographing the nude body, photographers generally prefer soft, diffused lighting, which prevents harsh, uneven skin tones and blemishes from showing. A diffuser card in front of the flash helps in this case.

Architecture

The SB-28's high power is excellent for interior architectural shots.

For interior spaces, use a wide-angle diffuser: Because limited space frequently requires the use of wide-angle lenses, the zoom head should be used in wide-angle position. The SB-28's 18/20mm diffuser panel is ideal for extreme wide-angle shots.

Optional auxiliary flash: Larger rooms with many angles may require the use of additional auxiliary, slave flash units to lighten distant corners (e.g., use SB-28 on-camera and SB-26 as the slave unit; see "TTL Flash With Non-TTL Slave").

Unnatural-Looking Faces

In the section "Portraits," you will find information on how to prevent excessively "washed-out" faces, rigid facial expressions, and tightly shut eyes when taking pictures of people.

Slide Duplication

Slide-duplicating devices: Slide duplication is a special application of macro photography. Basic duplicating devices are available for less than $100. The only disadvantage of simple duplicating devices is that the reproduction ratio is frequently slightly greater than 1:1, meaning that some of the original image is cut off. There are two options for 1:1 duplicates: A macro lens (such as AF Micro Nikkor 60mm/2.8 or 105mm/2.8) or a bellows unit with a slide-duplication attachment. The macro lens is best used on a copy stand, with the slide placed on a light table below. Slide holders are available for bellows units. Nikon, for example, has a PS-6 attachment for use with the PB-6 bellows. In addition to the bellows, a lens is required.

Films: Special slide duplicating film by Kodak (Kodak Ektachrome SE duplicating film, SO-366) should be used to make slide duplicates (dupes). Like many transparency films, the film is designed for Process E-6. It is recommended to be used with electronic flash and appropriate filtration. The use of standard slide film is not recommended for making dupes because the results generally will have too much contrast.

Basic flash exposure control: Most slide duplicating devices work with fixed apertures of approximately f/8 to f/16. Even when using a macro lens, you should use an aperture of approximately f/8 to f/11.

The basic brightness of the flash exposure can be varied in TTL flash mode. Or you can use fully manual flash mode by varying the distance between the flash unit and the slide or by inserting neutral density (ND) filters (in an emergency, tracing paper). With the SB-28, a distance of approximately 10 inches from the slide duplicating device is recommended.

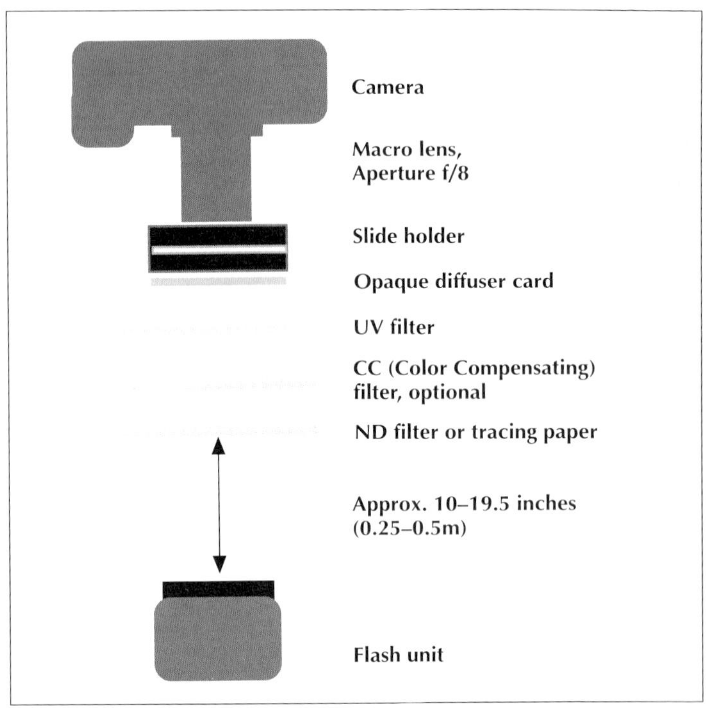

Typical slide duplication setup

Duplicating Slides in conventional TTL flash mode: Flash units are excellent for use in slide duplication. Unfortunately, there is one restriction: The low sensitivity of the Kodak Ektachrome slide duplicating film may possibly prevent the use of TTL flash control. It is probably best to take test exposures with a film speed setting of ISO 6 and conventional TTL control. Vary the "basic brightness" of the flash as previously described. The SB-28's red flash control LED will indicate if the exposure is not sufficient.

Varying TTL flash exposure with the SB-28: Ideal for use in slide duplication (camera permitting) is the compensation affecting only the flash in TTL mode. This allows you to vary the flash exposure between steps of +1 and -3. You can also use the exposure compensation on the camera.

Fully manual flash exposures: Of course, you can adapt the SB-28 to your slide duplicating device by using manual flash mode and by varying the output level in a series of test exposures.

Color filters: Be sure to read and follow the film manufacturer's recommendations/specifications packaged with the film. In addition, for best results and to fine-tune color rendition, use color-compensating (CC) gelatin-square filters.

Capturing Memories

Be it a birthday party, your child under the Christmas tree, or a service award banquet, most pictures are meant to capture memories.

Lenses: Generally, most people-pictures are taken from distances ranging from approximately 5 to 15 feet. Suitable lens focal lengths range from about 28mm to 100mm.
Recommendations: ISO 100 or ISO 200 films are always a good choice for use with the SB-28. In direct flash mode you should be careful because there may not be enough ambient light and the depth of field of the subject may decrease dramatically. Due to light fall-off, the foreground may be too light or the background too dark. Using *bounce* flash against a white ceiling usually works quite well. In my experience with practical applications, even standard TTL autoflash provides good results. An alternative would be to use a diffuser card on the SB-28 to create a less harsh gradient and softer, more diffuse light. See the section "Variable Stroboframe Flash Bracket."

Family: For detailed information, look under "Portraits."

Children: Photographs of children frequently appear posed or look like the children were forced into having their picture taken. By taking a greater number of pictures or preliminary flash shots, the atmosphere may be relaxed. For more information, see "Portraits" and "Red-Eye."

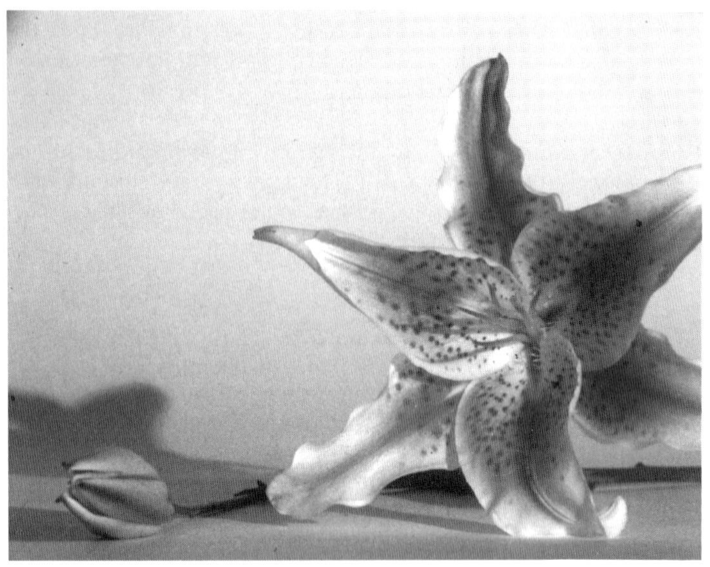

For this artistic close-up shot of a lily, the flash was used off-camera to cast side shadows, giving the photo a sense of depth.

Close-Up Photography With the SB-28

The vertical-tilt flash head of the SB-28 may be aligned at a downward angle of -7°. At extremely close ranges, the full light cone may no longer cover the subject. This should be used with on-camera flash when the subject is within 4–5 feet from the camera. (With N70/F70, N90/F90, and F5 cameras, the monitor preflash may be deactivated by slightly tilting the zoom head.)

Unrestricted Flash Exposures With TTL Autoflash

True macro-photographs are best taken with the SB-28 in an off-camera position using the SC-17 adapter cable and TTL auto fill-flash mode. Also, the Stroboframe LP macro flash bracket is practical because it can be aligned with the SB-28 at exactly the right angle relative to the lens in the close-up range.

Modifying the flash brightness: You can modify flash intensity slightly by attaching the 18/20mm diffuser panel to the front of

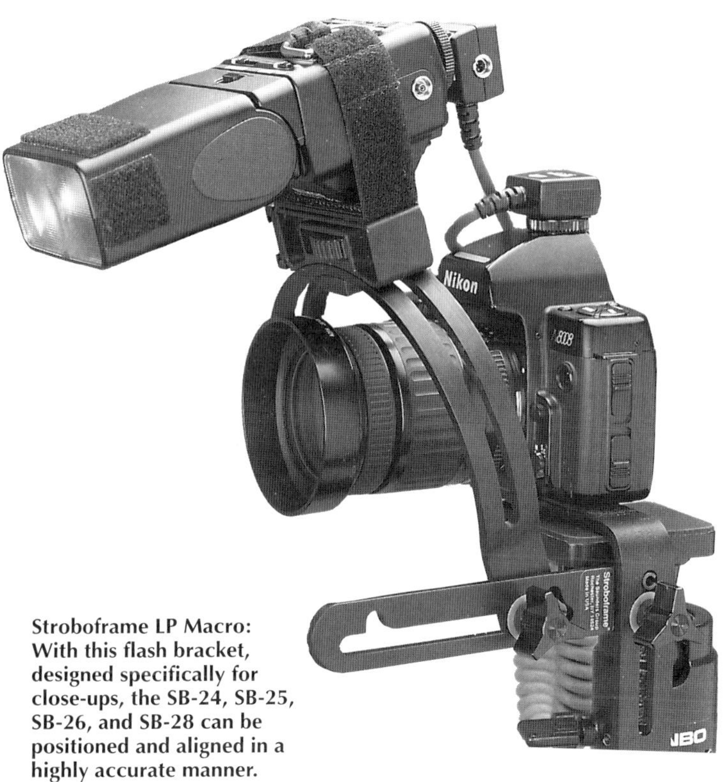

Stroboframe LP Macro: With this flash bracket, designed specifically for close-ups, the SB-24, SB-25, SB-26, and SB-28 can be positioned and aligned in a highly accurate manner.

the zoom head. If the flash still proves to be too bright in test exposures, it may be attenuated additionally by means of a neutral density filter or sheet of white typing paper.

Minimum aperture: Depending on the film sensitivity, Nikon recommends using a minimum aperture for flash distances less than 25 inches. If a larger aperture is selected, the TTL System may not have enough time to correctly adjust the flash.

Soft, shadow-free light using a light tent: See "Tabletop Exposures" for more information.

Portraits

Lenses: Portraits require careful illumination and are best shot with focal lengths of approximately 80mm to 105mm. This focal length range is ideal because, even with a head-and-shoulders shot, a subject distance of approximately 5 to 10 feet can be maintained for flexibility in lighting and composition. In addition, portraits made using this focal length range maintain a natural-looking perspective. Focal lengths less than 50mm often result in noticeable, unattractive distortion of facial features. Since a soft, out-of-focus background is usually preferred, a large aperture should be selected using aperture priority or manual mode. An additional advantage of the large aperture is that the image usually becomes slightly "softer," which often enhances appearance in a portrait.

Excessive contrast, partial overexposure: You can prevent flash portraits from appearing too contrasty or "washed out" by using bounce flash with a diffuser card or by using the wide-angle diffuser panel in front of the flash. In an emergency, a piece of tracing paper, which has been crunched and stuck to the flash head with tape, will also work. This is not really necessary for cameras with TTL auto fill-flash and the relatively "soft" SB-28 reflector, but it may add a slight additional improvement. (When using N70/F70, N90/F90, and F5 cameras with these diffusers, deactivate monitor preflash by light-tilting the zoom head.) Bounce flash, with the SB-28 using the pull-out diffuser card, is also effective. With this, you can add "catch-lights" in the model's eyes, provided the distance is not too great.

Red-eye reduction: To guard against red-eye, use the red-eye reduction option when shooting portraits.

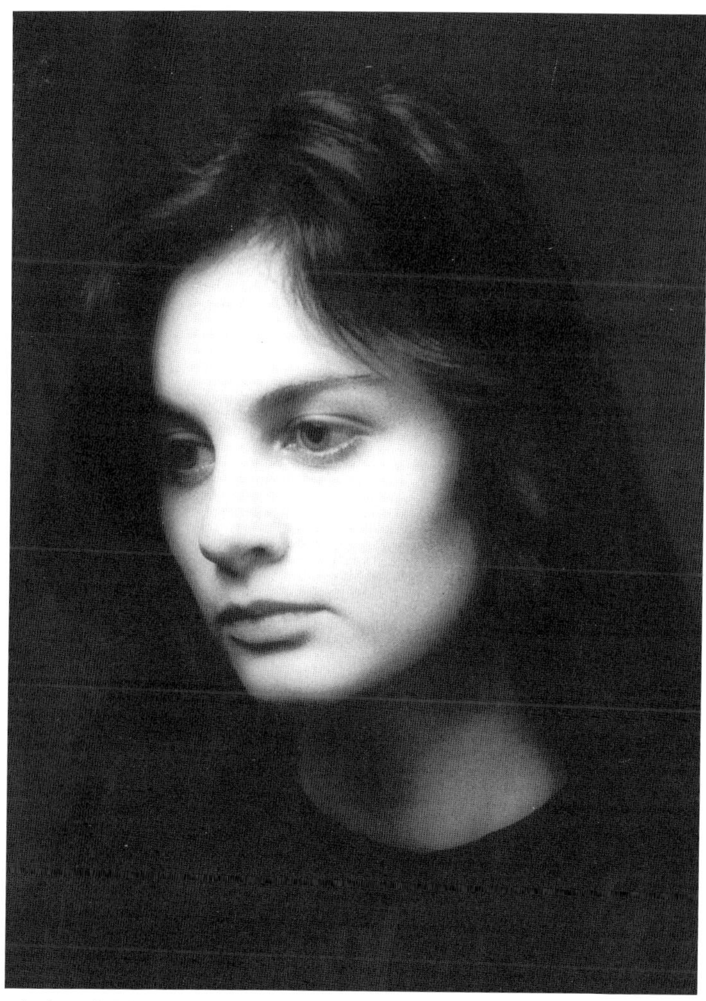

Flash and diffuser: A diffuser was attached to the flash unit and an additional, subtle diffuser filter (Tiffen®) was attached to the lens.
Photograph: Wolf Huber

Spatially Deep Subjects

Manual flash mode: You will quickly discover that very few subjects are flat; the vast majority have at least minimal depth. Imagine a long wedding banquet table. If you select the aperture according to the center of the table, the bride in the foreground will be too bright and the groom at the other end will be too dark, while only the relatively unimportant center is properly exposed. Bouncing the flash off the white ceiling in manual mode is a "game of chance" in this situation. To obtain the correct exposure would require bracketing. But that requires time which you probably don't have. Using TTL mode and bounce flash in this situation eliminates all of the hassle. When using this mode, as mentioned, the aperture is determined by the distance from flash to subject. But what aperture should you use?

TTL flash mode: Using this mode, the flash brightness on the subject will be metered (even with bounce flash), and properly exposed pictures will result.

Variation of the background brightness: Usually, spatial depth "swallows up" some of the light emitted by the flash. Depending on the combination of camera model and SB-28, this can be prevented in various ways. See the chapter *Flash Methods for Special Applications.*

Copy Photography

Copy stands: A stable copy stand is an absolute "must" for copy work. This assures that the film plane is parallel to the plane of the original. (You can check this and make fine adjustments, if necessary, with a bubble level.)

Flash unit setup: This is best done with two equally powered flash units mounted at a 45-degree angle. Diffusers in front of the flash units are also recommended in this application. The distance from the lights for subjects up to 8 x 11 inches should be about three feet. If you do not own two SB-28 units, the second unit may be any less powerful, simpler flash unit. Use it in manual mode. The

SB-28 can be matched to this unit by reducing the output level. The system is activated (see "Recommendations for Using TTL Multiflash Mode") by using SC-17 and SC-19 cords or a slave unit to trigger the second flash.

Red-Eye

Cause and cures: Notorious red-eye can be blamed on the camera-mounted flash unit. If the flash axis and lens axis are almost the same, the light reflected off the red retina at the rear of the eye becomes visible. If there is a significant distance between the lens and flash axes, however, this red light is reflected from the image area. Diffusing the flash is one solution, but it reduces flash intensity. A better alternative is to use a flash bracket, such as a Stroboframe bracket, which raises the flash high above the camera. The flash-axis change effectively eliminates red-eye.

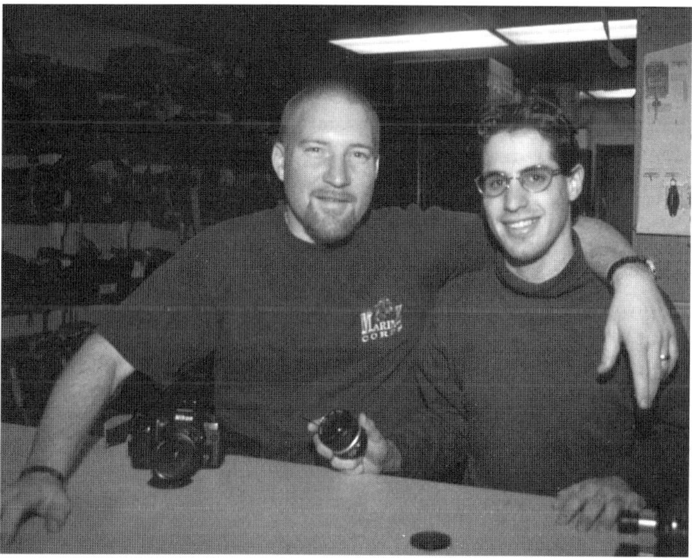

Red-eye can be a problem, especially if the subject is looking directly into the lens. Use red-eye reduction or move the flash off-camera, away from the lens axis, to help eliminate red-eye.

This works fairly well, but most professionals rely on other methods in addition to preflash. See the section "Variable Stroboframe Flash Bracket."

Product Photography

Pictures of objects: No photographer should claim "artistic freedom" with product shots. Whatever needs to be shown must be visible! As a rule, this calls for extremely sharp images, extended depth of field, and uniform illumination. Therefore, studio-type pictures of objects require high flash output because the necessary image sharpness is best achieved by using low-sensitivity films and relatively small apertures.

Illumination: Uniform illumination is important because shadows and high contrast lighting will interfere with the finished result. You should use shadows for artistic expression only when you have mastered proper illumination.

Using one SB-28 flash: A cleverly used, high-power flash unit, such as the SB-28, will frequently yield amazing results. For example, by using a studio umbrella, the flash may be transformed into a large-area, soft light source. An additional white or silver reflector (the Domke® company makes some of the most versatile) can help lighten shadows.

Multiple flash units: You can work even more precisely with several flash units (three units in a studio will cover most lighting challenges). Normally, the strongest flash is fired nearly straight-on as the main light source. Specialized diffuser panels, such as those made by Domke, do wonders with otherwise harsh lighting. A second, weaker unit can be used as background illumination or as a bottom light, and the third can be positioned to create accents. Since modeling lights are very useful but somewhat extravagant for a basic studio, two inexpensive clamp reflector sockets with 60-watt bulbs are an economical alternative.

Helpful hint: Build a light tent out of tracing paper or diffusion material and use one flash unit on either side.

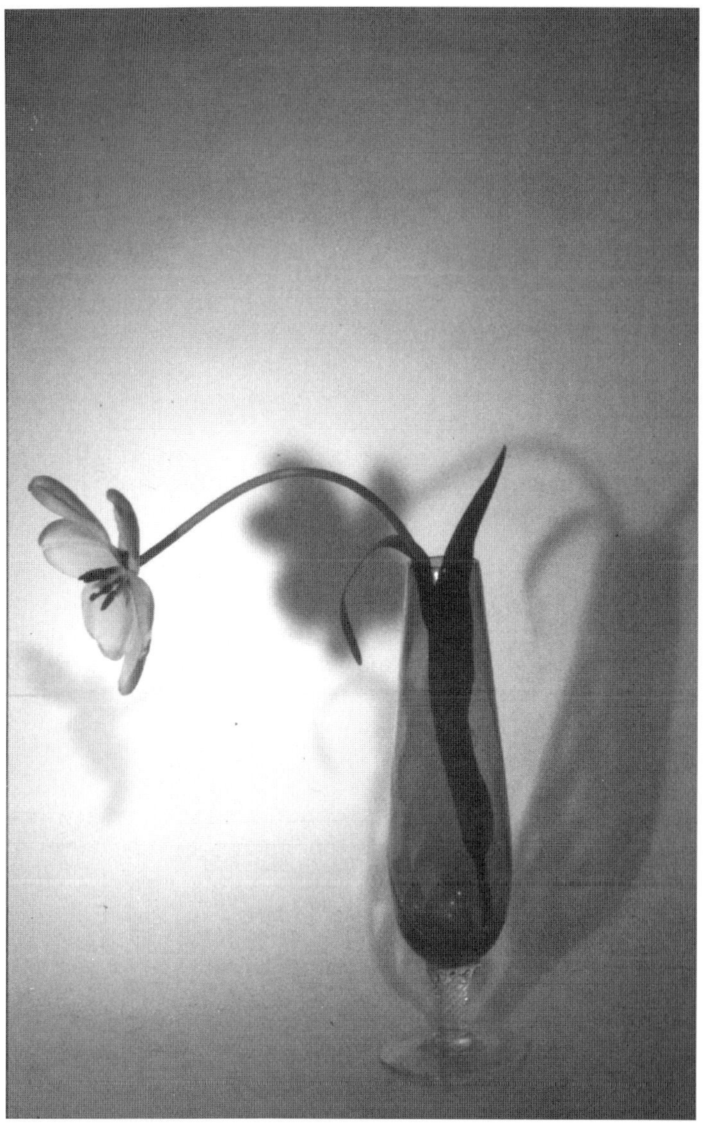

A simple yet elegant studio shot required a piece of seamless background paper, two flash units, and the flower and vase.

Sports and Action

Lenses and films: Generally, flash photography is strictly forbidden in sporting arenas. If you are in a situation where flash is permitted, use a telephoto lens (approximately 180mm to 400mm) and fast film. When using a flash, most cameras can accommodate films with film speeds of up to about ISO 1000. But even with fast films, it becomes rapidly obvious that the SB-28's output is sometimes inadequate at distances exceeding 100 feet. Unfortunately, Nikon does not include a light-intensifying telephoto attachment with the SB-28.

Tabletop Exposures

Basically, the principles are similar to those described earlier in photographing objects.

Light tents: One special way of creating uniform illumination when shooting smaller objects is to create a light tent of tracing paper or diffusion material and illuminate the subject with one or more flash units positioned at an appropriate distance. It's best to use one flash unit on each side of the tent as described in the section "Copy Photography." However, unlike copy work, TTL control may be used, and the flash units do not have to be equal in output. In spite of the light tent (or more accurately because of it) the more powerful flash unit will cast only a weak shadow, which will favorably enhance the three-dimensional appearance of the objects.

The Basics of Flash Technology

Thanks to autoflash, anyone can take flash pictures without tedious computations. Nevertheless, most photographers will find knowledge of the fundamentals of using flash helpful. For example, do you know that an aperture of f/8 with a guide number of 32 will reach only a ridiculous 10 inches farther than the same aperture with a guide number of 30? Or do you know why the N90/F90's 3D-autoflash with the SB-28 produces better results than the F4 or N8008/F-801 in matrix-balanced autoflash mode?

Flash Output, Duration, and Guide Number

Light energy is a product of flash output and duration: The degree of brightness of a subject illuminated by a flash unit is a function of the output of the flash unit. The resulting photographic exposure is a function of the duration of this output. Therefore, the energy emitted by the flash is calculated as the product of flash output and duration.

Brightness decreases with distance: Both the energy emitted by the flash unit and its proportion reaching the subject are important to the final exposure. Therefore, the distance of the flash unit from the subject is critical. Almost all light sources emit light at a specific angle (cone) of illumination. The area covered by this cone increases with increasing distance. This means that the same brightness will be distributed over an increasingly larger area. Effectively, because of this, an object will receive less light the farther it is located from the flash unit. In short, flash units are subject to the law which states: Brightness decreases in proportion to the square of the distance.

Distance	3 ft (.9m)	6 ft (1.8m)	9 ft (2.7m)	12 ft (3.7m)	18 ft (5.5m)	27 ft (8.2m)
Relative brightness	1/1	1/4	1/9	1/16	1/36	1/81

Guide number: The guide number is a value which takes into consideration flash energy, the relationship between brightness and distance, and film sensitivity. It has been sensibly defined so that it considers only values which are important in practical applications, namely aperture and distance.

Guide number, aperture, and distance: If the distance from the subject has been predetermined and the guide number corresponding to the film sensitivity is known, you can determine the correct aperture quite easily. This answers the question, "What aperture should I select to obtain the correct exposure for a subject at a given distance?"

Aperture = guide number ÷ distance

Distance, flash shooting range: You can determine the shooting range of your flash unit at a certain aperture. You compute the distance at which the pre-determined aperture and flash guide number provide the correct flash exposure as follows:

Distance = guide number ÷ aperture

Examples of computation: For example, a flash unit using a guide number of 96 will correctly expose a subject at a distance of 6 feet with an aperture of f/16 (96/6). At a distance of 12 feet, the aperture would have to be f/8 (96/12). Conversely, if a subject at a distance of 24 feet is properly exposed with an aperture of f/4(96/24), the correct aperture at a distance of 3 feet would be f/32(96/3). Most flash units have a computation disk or slide which indicates the distance range at a given aperture, or the correct aperture for a given distance. (In manual mode, the SB-28's LCD will automatically indicate the appropriate distance for a given aperture.)

Guide number and film sensitivity: The guide number indication normally refers to a film sensitivity of ISO 100. More sensitive films give a higher guide number, so the distance range increases at a given aperture. Each time the film sensitivity is doubled, the applicable guide number is multiplied by 1.4. (If the guide number was 40 with ISO 100, the guide number will be 56 with ISO 200.) Therefore, if the distance from the subject is the same, you may reduce the aperture by one f/stop when the film sensitivity is doubled. This is also illustrated on the flash unit's display panel.

Guide number and zoom flash heads: With zoom flash heads, the illumination angle is modified so that the angle of view of different focal lengths will be covered by the flash. You accomplish this by adjusting the position of the flash head diffuser relative to the flash tube. By adjusting the zoom head, the flash energy is concentrated on a smaller angle of illumination. The following applies: The smaller the angle of illumination (long focal lengths), the greater the guide number; the greater the angle of illumination (short focal lengths), the smaller the guide number.

Guide number in autoflash mode: In automatic flash mode, the flash guide number corresponds to the maximum energy output when the flash is in manual mode. However, if the subject distance requires flash energy which is lower than this guide number, the energy or duration of the flash is reduced by the autoflash system. The automatic system has saved us from having to make troublesome computations with guide numbers and apertures.

Guide number with multiple flash: When working with several flash units simultaneously, the combined guide number is important regardless of which flash mode is used. With similar direction of illumination and uniform distance from the subject, the combined guide number of the individual flash units can be determined by squaring and adding the individual guide numbers (GN), and by ratifying the sum.

Combined guide number = $\sqrt{(GN_1)^2 + (GN_2)^2 + \dots (GN_n)^2}$

Aperture with a combination of several flash units: If several flash units are used at different distances, it makes sense to compute the appropriate lens aperture, which will be the result of the combined action of each aperture (AP) for each flash unit.

Combined aperture = $\sqrt{(AP_1)^2 + (AP_2)^2 + \dots (AP_n)^2}$

Different flash distances with autoflash mode: There is no simple formula for this. For best results with studio flash, take a reading on the subject with a flash meter and shoot test exposures. This way the effect of the individual flash units and their combined effect may be tested step-by-step.

Autoflash Modes

To appreciate the limitations and advantages of different autoflash modes, it is helpful to understand how they work.

Flash Output Control

Principle: If the autoflash system determines the distance from the subject and the selected aperture before firing, it will simply adjust its output accordingly before firing. A flash with a guide number of 138, an aperture of f/8, and a distance from the subject of 13 feet would automatically be adjusted downward to a guide number of 105, and at 10 feet to a guide number of 80, etc. To my knowledge, complex electronic control of the actual flash output is presently not used by any camera/autoflash mode (instead they simply adjust the duration of the flash). However, there are some studio-type flash systems which permit manual pre-selection of the flash output while the duration of the flash remains the same.

Confusing use of flash *output* and flash *intensity*: In its publications, Nikon frequently uses the concepts of controlling or adjusting the "flash output" or "flash power," even though "flash energy" is meant. In this book, I have at times used this "simplified" language. To my knowledge, all Nikon SLR cameras and flash units control the flash energy via manual presetting or automatic control of the duration of the flash.

Autoflash With Distance Measurement

In autoflash mode, the aperture and duration are computed from the guide number and the AF distance: You can estimate the appropriate duration of the flash when you know the flash output, aperture, and exact distance from the main subject. (This is the same in fully manual flash mode.) The 3D matrix autoflash mode of the N70/F70, N90/F90, and F5 cameras (see below) uses the distance information provided by AF lenses in conjunction with monitor preflashes.

Advantage: Because this method is independent of the reflectance of the surroundings outside the picture, you can obtain very precisely exposed pictures.

Disadvantage: Because the flash output is calibrated with respect to the *average* reflectance of the subject's surroundings, exposure errors may occur. If the surroundings absorb more than the *average* amount of light, the subject becomes too dark. If the surroundings reflect more than the average amount of light, the subject becomes too light.

Medical Nikkor lens: Nikon has used this method for a long time with its medical Nikkor lens, where the manual focus adjustment is coupled by electromechanical means with the aperture and flash duration control. As a result, extremely accurate flash exposures are obtained in the critical close-up range.

Control of Flash Duration Based on Reflected Light

Non-TTL autoflash. The possible duration of a flash exposure ranges between approximately 1/200 and 1/50000 second (1/830 and 1/8700 second for the SB-28). The principle behind non-TTL autoflash mode is the automatic control of this duration as a function of exposure conditions. These conventional autoflash units have an integrated external photo sensor, which measures the light reflected by the subject during the flash exposure. The flash control is totally independent of the camera.

TTL flash control: In this mode, the light from the flash reflected off the subject is measured by the camera.

Non-TTL Automatic (Sensor) Flash

A misleading concept: Sometimes improperly labeled as "computerized flash," this concept dates back to a time when every manufacturer offering clever electronics in flash units identified them, for marketing purposes, as having an internal "computer." Only more advanced units such as the SB-25, SB-26, and SB-28, have integrated microprocessors and are "genuine" computerized flash units.

Non-TTL automatic flash clearly defined: Non-TTL autoflash refers to flash duration control via the sensor in the flash unit. This is independent of the camera. On Nikon flash units, including the SB-28, this function is identified by "A."

Operation: Let's look at a typical automatic flash unit, which has a guide number of 136 at full power and at a duration of 1/1000 second (an aperture of f/8 and a range of 17 feet). If, after releasing and firing the flash, too much light is reflected because the main subject is only 10 feet away, the sensor will automatically switch off the flash and reduce the flash duration to 1/2000 second. This results in a well-exposed picture. The main drawback of non-TTL autoflash is that the angle covered by the flash's sensor frequently does not coincide with the image angle of the lens. The sensor, located on the flash unit, has a fixed measuring angle of approximately 60°. This angle approximates the field of view of a 35mm lens. Because of this, the use of wide-angle lenses with a larger angle of view and telephoto lenses with a considerably narrower image angle may easily result in incorrect flash exposures. Either too little light reflected by the subject may be detected or light reflected from areas not even in the final picture may register. In addition, most non-TTL automatic flash units work with a rather restricted aperture range.

Standard TTL Flash

Principle of TTL flash metering: In TTL autoflash mode, the flash exposure is measured through the lens (TTL). The mirror is flipped up, the aperture closes down to the correct value, the shutter curtain opens fully, and then the flash is fired. During the period when the shutter is open, the flash metering cell on the camera bottom (see diagram) measures the light reflected off the film and regulates the flash duration as a result of this reading.

The Optical Path of a TTL-Controlled Flash Exposure

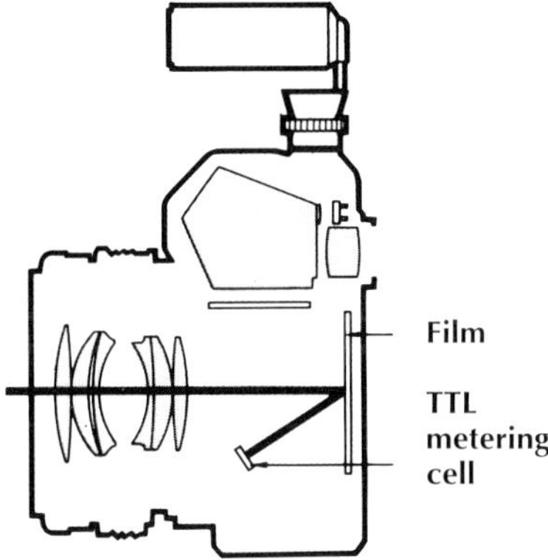

Built-in consideration of angle of view and aperture: Compared with conventional non-TTL automatic flash units, TTL flash control has the advantage that it covers the image angle of the subject accurately. Also, lens converters or filters are automatically taken into consideration. In TTL flash mode, the aperture set on the lens is of relatively little consequence because a wide range of apertures are automatically catered for by adjusting the flash duration.

Limitations of TTL Flash

Electronic limitations: As with any type of electronic instrument control, TTL flash has its limitations. An extremely short time is required for the camera's electronics to measure, compute, and send to flash unit's thyristor the "deactivate" signal. The thyristor acts as power switch. It also has an intrinsic switching time. If the required flash duration is shorter than this computing and switching time, overexposed images will result. Whenever the distance from the subject is very small and the aperture is very large (using the guide number of the flash unit and the film speed), TTL-controlled flash exposures can possibly be overexposed.

Limits of standard TTL autoflash: Whenever (for example, with flash exposures in total darkness or with fill-flash) the main subject does not fill the picture and is not at a uniform distance, only a fraction of the light will be reflected by the subject. The remainder of the light emitted by the flash is lost in the background "next to" the main subject. The TTL autoflash attempts to overcome this by prolonging the duration of the flash. The result is an overexposed subject, especially, when it's in the foreground.

Limits of standard TTL auto fill-flash: When there's a noticeable amount of ambient light or the subject is definitely backlit, expose the scene with an appropriate combination of shutter speed and aperture to achieve natural-looking results. This does not occur automatically with conventional TTL auto fill-flash.

Manual exposure adjustment and flash compensation: On advanced N8008/F-801, F4, F5, and N90/F90 cameras, you can make manual flash corrections via the SB-28's manual flash compensation function. (This is applicable also to SB-25 and SB-26.) In manual exposure mode, the aperture and, depending on the camera model, shutter speed may be adjusted to the brightness of the ambient light and background.

Unusual reflectance of the subject: Problems arise with subjects exhibiting unusual reflecting power or the lack of it. Autoflash is calibrated (as are most exposure meters) for a subject with medium reflecting power. This calibration to 18% (medium) gray may have a negative effect on flash metering and control. Naturally dark subjects with low reflecting power will be lightened automatically and reproduced in an unnaturally light manner. Conversely, very light subjects with high reflecting power will be photographed in an unnaturally gray or dark manner. The bride in white in front of the white wall will record too dark. The black cat in front of the black car will record too light. If you want to do better than the autoflash, you must set the flash unit and the camera to manual flash mode. If the subject reflects light in a highly irregular manner, you should not rely on automatic flash. Ultimate perfection is possible only using fully manual flash and metering by hand. Only the N90/F90, F5, or N70/F70 with TTL multi-sensor, monitor preflash, and 3D matrix control in combination with the SB-28, can handle many of these problem subjects automatically.

Simple TTL Auto Fill-Flash
Definition: This automatic feature makes an automatic preflash correction but does not sufficiently consider continuous light or background brightness when determining aperture and shutter speed (compared with matrix-balanced TTL auto fill-flash).

Exposure metering method affects only ambient light: The automatic flash features of all current Nikon cameras work with a selected camera exposure metering method (matrix, center-weighted, or spot). This selection affects only the measurement of ambient light. TTL flash control is completely independent and always has a slightly center-weighted bias (with the exception of the N70/F70, N90/F90, and F5 using TTL multi-sensor flash metering). Some Nikon cameras with auto fill-flash also have an automatic minus correction of the flash exposure when set for spot (not F4 or F5) or center-weighted ambient light metering (typically minus 2/3). This automatically counteracts too much flash exposure of the foreground.

Center-weighted TTL auto fill-flash: This slightly confusing description might imply that the flash is metered in a center-weighted manner before actual exposure to determine the shutter speed and the aperture for the ambient light level. In automatic exposure modes, such as aperture priority, shutter priority, or program, the subject in the foreground is usually over-evaluated for ambient light while the background remains under-evaluated. As a result, auto fill-flash with automatic program or aperture mode often results in an unnaturally light background exposure. Center-weighted ambient-light metering should therefore be used only with older cameras that do not feature matrix metering or when an AF lens is not available for modern AF cameras. The best procedure is the center-weighted TTL auto fill-flash with manual adjustment for the background (see below).

Spot metering: The same reservations apply as with center-weighted metering. In many cases this is even more critical. Watch F4 and F5 cameras as they revert to standard TTL flash.

Targeted adaptation of the background: Using TTL auto fill-flash and manual camera exposure adjustment, a targeted adaptation of

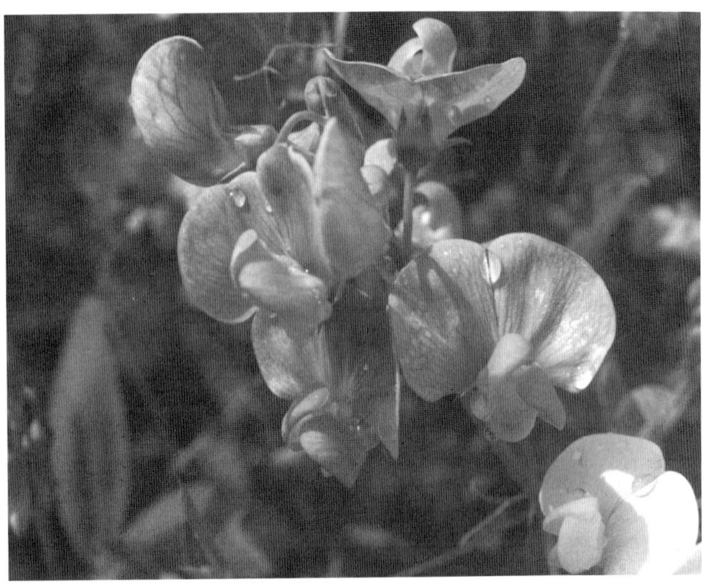

Matrix-balanced fill-flash brightened up the close-up of these flowers.

the background by spot or center-weighted metering permits a precise adjustment of both foreground and background brightness. The minus correction of TTL auto fill-flash creates a subtle lightening of the foreground.

Matrix metering: Only matrix metering automatically considers surrounding light and subject contrast (see below).

Matrix-Balanced Automatic Fill-Flash

Definition of "matrix:" The term "matrix" often causes confusion. It applies to a multi-pattern evaluation of the brightness and contrast in a scene. This process then provides exposure information to the camera's multiprocessor. Matrix metering analyzes the brightness in a scene and refers the *light pattern* seen to a stored memory of thousands of potential light patterns. It then selects an exposure "intelligently" from that evaluation. In comparison, center-weighted or spot metering simply calculate an exposure value to reproduce a metered area as 18% gray. In any case, the camera can automatically select aperture and/or shutter speed as needed, based on the exposure mode ("P," "S," or "A"). If the camera is in TTL fill-flash mode, the flash exposure will be reduced somewhat during the exposure for a more natural-looking result. This is based on a reference value provided by the camera's TTL flash sensor. In matrix metering, the camera may choose flash reduction over a controlled range (about a stop) to match the brightness and contrast characteristics of the original scene. Since matrix is an "intelligent" meter it can provide the information the microprocessor needs to choose the flash exposure compensation. More accurately, matrix "influences" flash exposure, but does not, strictly speaking, control it.

Exposure metering and flash compensation before exposure, with TTL control during exposure: In this mode, with the N6006/ F-601, N8008/ F-801, and F4 cameras, the camera's computer links the automatic features of the ambient light exposure mode with the methods of TTL-controlled flash metering. In practice, this means that in autoflash mode and matrix metering, both background light and subject contrast are taken into consideration. Along with this exposure metering, the autoflash selects the aperture and/or the shutter speed before the flash is fired, and then adjusts the duration of the flash based on the light reflected off the film during the TTL flash exposure. This type of autoflash may be activated in all exposure modes with automatic aperture or shutter priority, and program modes as well as manual exposure mode. However, matrix-balanced flash mode is most effective only with automatic program mode because the full range of shutter speeds and apertures is accessible automatically

Matrix control of various situations: Depending on total brightness and contrast, matrix-balanced autoflash evaluates the existing light and selects aperture, shutter speed, and flash duration. A distinction may be made among the following borderline cases of automatic exposure and flash control:

- *Extremely dark, any contrast:* The camera's computer automatically sets the aperture and shutter speed appropriate for the brightness measured in the central segment. At the same time, the computer makes a definite minus correction to prevent overexposure.

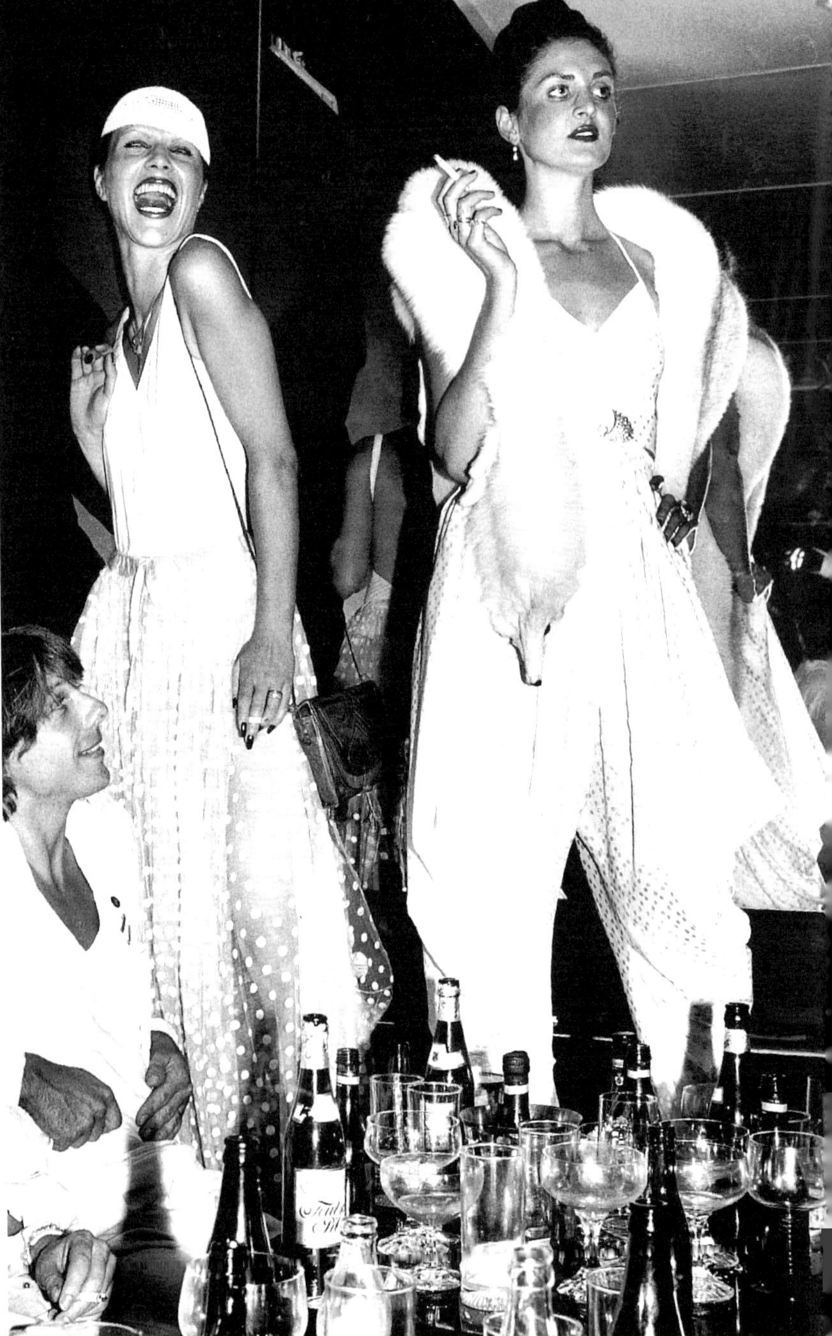

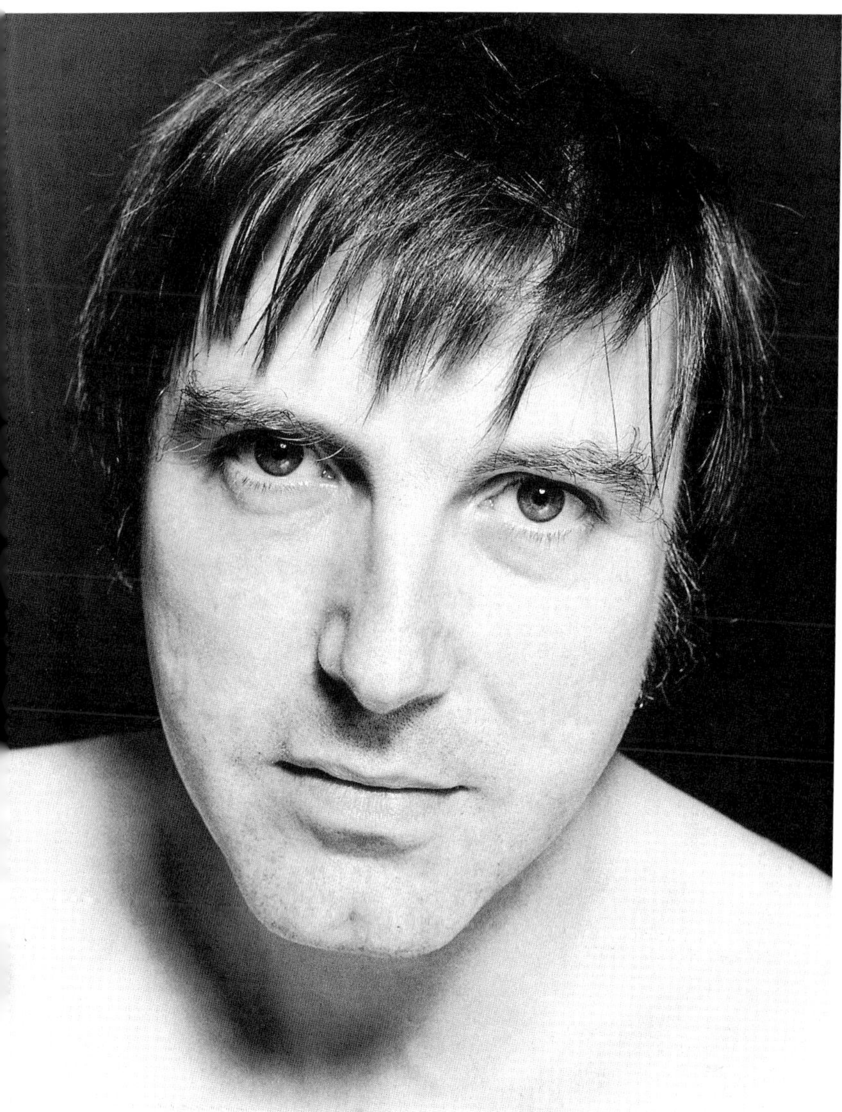

For this portrait, a studio flash set-up has been used.
Photograph: Wolf Huber

This action flash photo was shot with good TTL-metering. Brightness and contrast were enhanced during film development and printing.
Photograph: Rudolf Dietrich

- *Moderately dark, any contrast:* The camera's computer automatically sets the aperture and shutter speed appropriate for the darkest image area. At the same time, the computer makes a definite minus correction to prevent the foreground from becoming too light.
- *"Normal" dark, any contrast:* The camera's computer automatically sets the aperture and shutter speed appropriate for the average image brightness. At the same time, the computer makes a definite minus correction to prevent the foreground from becoming too light.
- *"Normal" light, low contrast:* The camera's computer automatically sets the aperture and shutter speed appropriate for the lightest image area. At the same time, the computer makes a definite minus correction to prevent the foreground from becoming too light.
- *"Normal" light, medium to low contrast:* The camera's computer automatically sets the aperture and shutter speed appropriate for the lighter image areas. At the same time, the computer makes moderate to significant minus corrections to the flash.
- *"Normal" light, high contrast:* The camera's computer automatically sets the aperture and shutter speed appropriate for the lightest image area. At the same time, the computer makes a slight minus correction to the flash because there is not much likelihood the foreground will be unnaturally light.

In each case, the flash duration is further controlled based on the light reflected by the surface of the film while the shutter is open.

From Normal Flash to Fill-Flash

Flash exposures in total darkness: Traditionally, TTL autoflash is based on the determination of a guide number corresponding to the aperture and/or flash duration, and distance. In total darkness, this may still be true to some extent. However, "normal" flash pictures usually look like typical "flash" pictures. You can attain a better balance with the foreground only by making minus corrections to the flash duration and plus corrections to the background.

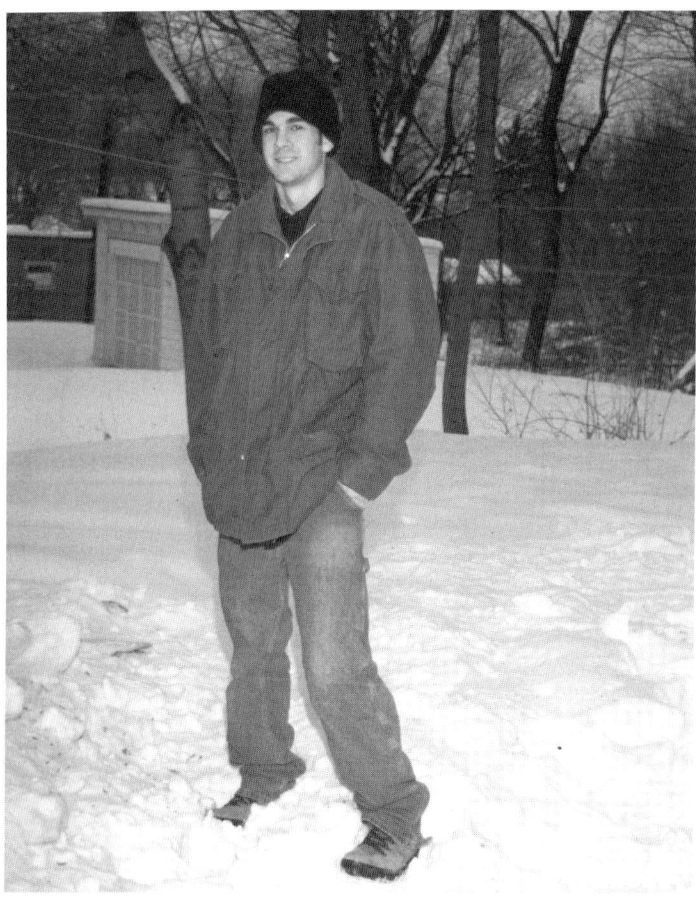

To retain a scene's atmospheric lighting, such as this evening winter sky, set the flash to underexpose slightly and increase the ambient light exposure. This will soften and balance the flash exposure on the subject with the light on the background.

Existing-light, fill-flash exposures: If there is noticeable existing light (e.g., outdoors at dusk or incandescent light in a room), pictures taken with conventional autoflash will appear unnaturally overexposed. Only a minus correction of the flash duration and an aperture opening appropriate for the existing light, as well as a relatively fast shutter speed, will provide "atmosphere."

Optical Paths of Different Systems for Determining Sharpness and Exposure (N90s/F90X)

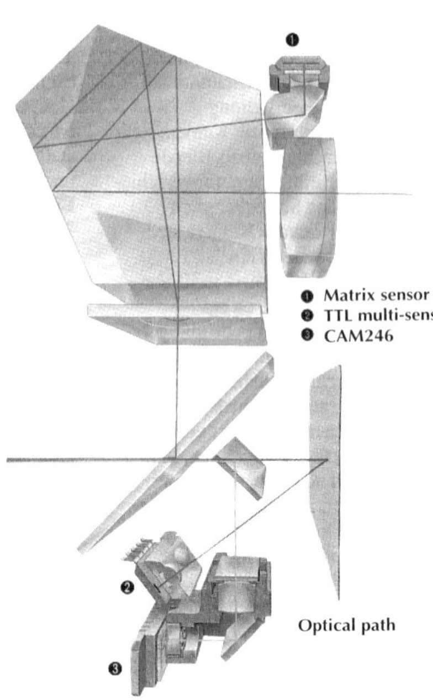

1. Shutter curtain
2. Bottom of the mirror box
3. Condenser lenses
4. TTL multi-sensor

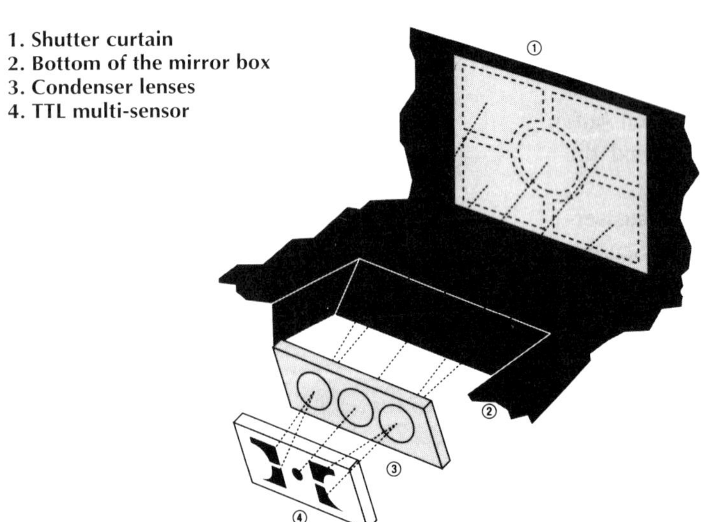

Multi-Sensor Flash Metering in the N90s/F90X

Autoflash
With Monitor
Preflash:

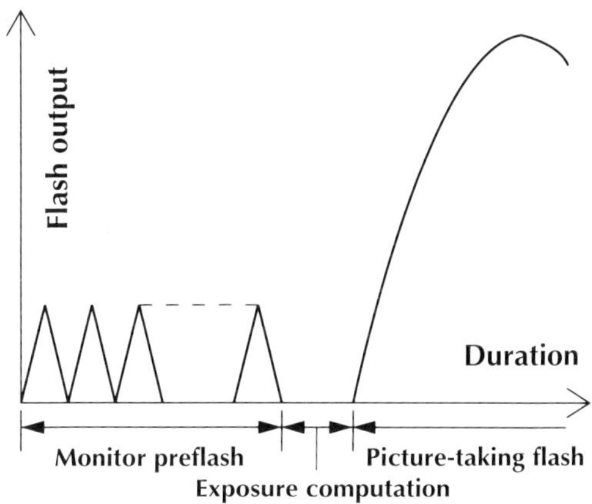

Backlit fill-flash exposures: In this case, the aperture and shutter speed must be adjusted for the background brightness. Flash compensation for the foreground will provide natural-looking pictures.

Smooth transition of matrix control: In contrast to standard TTL flash control, matrix balance in flash mode will automatically weigh all existing conditions.

Matrix-Balanced TTL Multi-Sensor Fill-Flash

Presently, you can use this method only with N70/F70, N90/F90, and F5 cameras with an AF Nikkor lens and any TTL flash unit. Normal matrix control occurs when using a preset aperture and/or shutter speed and an automatic preliminary compensation of the flash duration. After firing the flash, TTL control takes effect based on five-field multi-sensor metering. Because the N90/F90's computer considers those segments, which report unusually intense or unusually low light, the multi-sensor corrects extreme reflectance particularly well. Therefore, in multi-sensor autoflash mode, a subject-specific fine correction of the flash during the actual exposure occurs in addition to the subject-specific pre-selection of aperture, shutter speed, and flash duration.

Multi-Sensor Control With Additional Monitor Preflash

When the SB-28 is used with N70/F70, N90/F90, and F5 cameras, the flash unit emits a series of invisible preflashes, which are evaluated by the multi-sensor before the shutter release is depressed fully. As a result, information on the spatial distribution and the reflectance of the main subject and the background is relayed to the autoflash system. The computer, if necessary, then performs subject-specific preliminary compensation of the flash duration in addition to the matrix meter information.

3D Matrix Control

When using type D-AF Nikkor lenses, the autoflash system of the mentioned cameras considers the distance from the subject and the sharpness of the center of the picture while the shutter is released. This is done roughly in the following steps:

- **Conventional matrix metering:** The computer adjusts aperture, shutter speed, and preliminary flash compensation according to matrix metering prior to firing.
- **Comparison with a theoretical flash adjustment value based on the distance measurement:** The computer compares a previously determined flash exposure value (derived from guide number, aperture, and preliminary flash correction) with a theoretical value resulting from the distance and, if necessary, readjusts the preset flash exposure.
- **Focus check for off-center subjects:** At the time of firing, the computer recognizes if the center of the image is out of focus, image section has changed, and/or main subject is no longer in the center. In these cases, the computer sends the command to the TTL multi-sensor to reduce the emphasis of the measured central field during the actual flash exposure.
- **Monitor preflash for final, fine preliminary correction of the flash:** These measuring flashes (with SB-25, SB-26, SB-27, and SB-28 only) determine extreme reflectance conditions in the surrounding areas and result in an additional fine-tuning of the flash output. The computer then determines the weighting of multi-sensor metering while the flash is being fired.
- **TTL multi-sensor control during exposure:** The last fine compensation and final determination of the flash duration takes place by the five-field multi-sensor during the actual flash exposure.

Flash Synchronization

Definition

For complete exposure of the film frame, the flash must be fired when the focal-plane shutter is fully opened across the entire width of the image. In the case of the N90/F90, this occurs at shutter speeds of 1/250 second or longer. If the flash is fired before the shutter is fully opened (at speeds faster than 1/250 second) partial, striped, or even completely unexposed pictures will result. Generally, this is not a problem with modern Nikon cameras because the camera will not select a shutter speed faster than the maximum available sync speed in any of the automatic modes (except with the N90/F90, and F5, with SB-25, SB-26, or SB-28 on "FP").

Slow Synchronization

Years ago, flash release was superfluous with slower shutter speeds. This frequently caused double exposures due to the short-term flash and the additional long-term ambient light exposure. Any movement resulted in a blurred image superimposed on the sharp flash image. Most times this is unappealing, and only occasionally "artistic." However, it is possible to place a non-moving subject, exposed with flash, in front of a properly exposed existing-light background if the shutter speed is selected carefully (at normal shutter speeds there would be a black background). This is why some newer cameras, such as the N6006/F-601, N70/F70, N90/F90, and F5, feature an automatic "SLOW" function which allows the use of shutter speeds up to 30 seconds in all automatic flash modes. Other cameras permit the pre-selection of slower shutter speeds by combining TTL auto fill-flash with manual exposure adjustment.

First and Second Shutter Curtain Synchronization

With the fastest flash sync speed of 1/250 second, it makes no difference whether the flash is fired precisely after the complete opening of the first shutter curtain or *only* when the second curtain begins to move. The firing point is the same, namely, when the first shutter curtain has stopped and the second one has started. With slower shutter speeds, however, synchronization with the first curtain causes the exposure by existing light to occur *after* the flash is fired. With second shutter curtain ("REAR") sync, however, the existing-light exposure takes place *before* the flash is fired.

You can see the difference when photographing moving objects; they will have natural-looking motion blurs only in "REAR" mode. The SB-28 can be synchronized with the second shutter curtain when used with most modern Nikon cameras.

High-speed synchronization "FP": Currently, this feature is available only with the N90/F90 or F5 and the SB-25, SB-26, or SB-28. With normal brightness, extremely fast shutter speeds, combined with fill-flash, completely freeze a moving object. Extremely fast sync speeds may be used with fill-flash and large apertures to offset a flash-exposed, backlit subject in front of a normally bright, blurred background. This would not be possible in normal, automatic fill-flash mode because normal shutter speeds would make the background far too light. For these situations, the N90/F90 and F5 offer high-speed synchronization "FP" at up to 1/4000 second in manual mode in combination with the SB-25, SB-26, and SB-28.

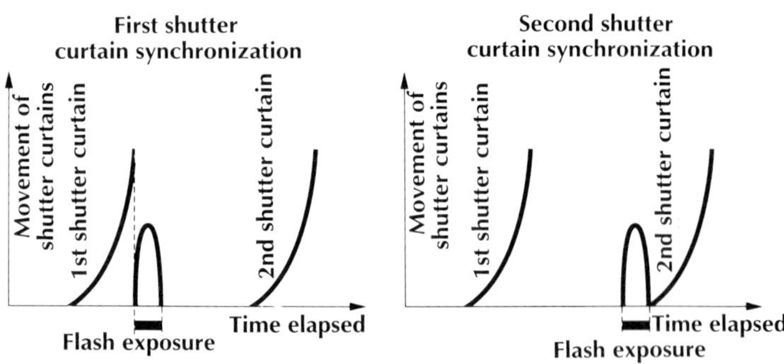

Representation of First and Second Shutter Curtain Synchronization

Procedure for high-speed flash "FP": With conventional flash sync, a single flash is fired shortly after the first or second curtain has opened. In "FP" mode with the N90/F90 or F5, the opening of the first shutter curtain causes the SB-28 (also SB-25 and SB-26) to trigger an uninterrupted sequence of short, high-frequency flash pulses. While the slotted opening of the shutter curtain sweeps over the film, the subject receives continuous flash exposure. This action distributes the total flash output over many flashes, which do not expose the entire image but only the respective shutter strip. This decreases the effective flash output, causing the guide number to also drop significantly. TTL flash control is not possible with "FP;" the camera and flash must be adjusted manually.

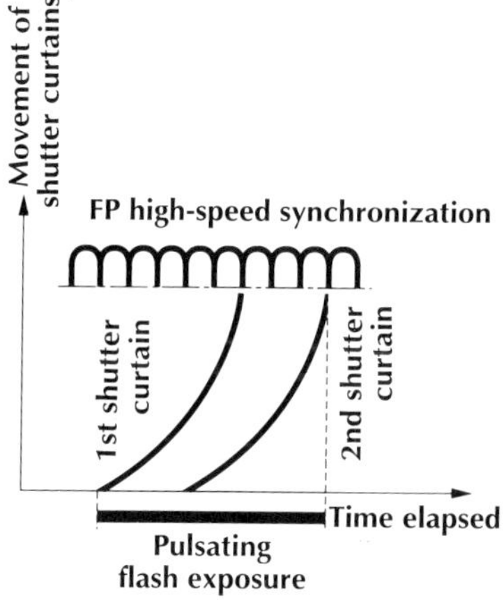

High-Speed Synchronization "FP"

Notes

Magic Lantern Guides

...take you beyond the camera's instruction manual.

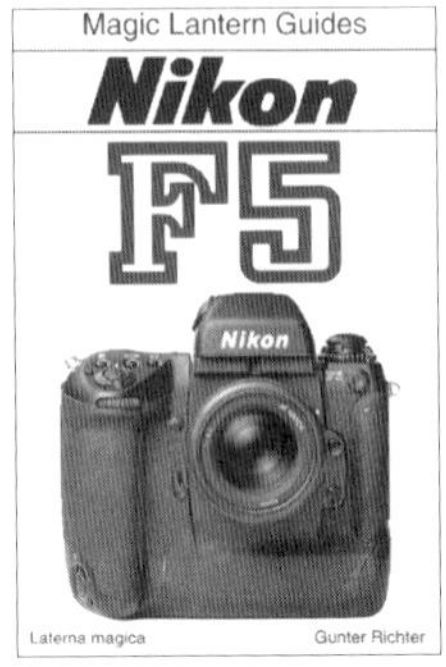

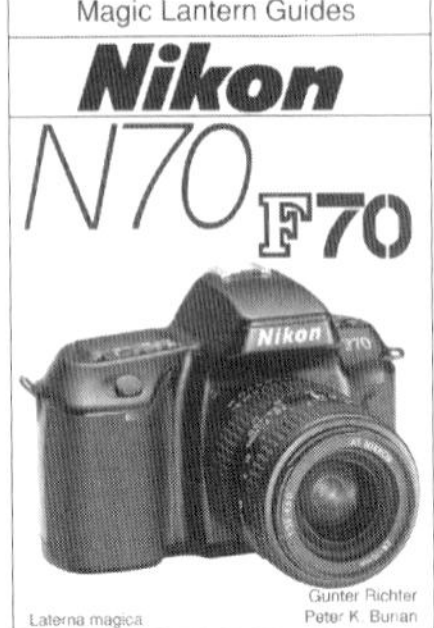

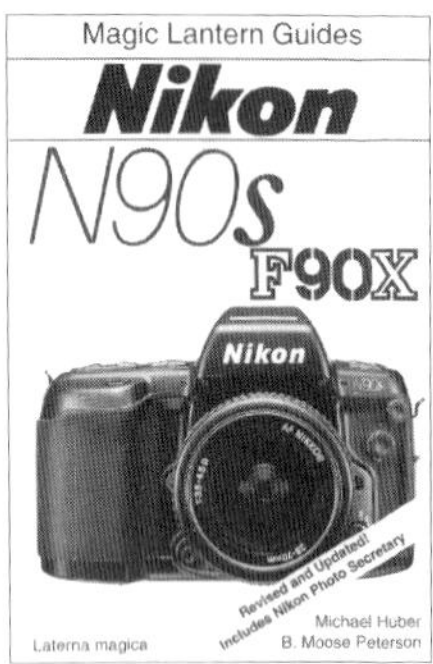

The world's most popular camera guides; available for most popular cameras and equipment.

The Nikon Field Guide

A Photographer's Portable Reference

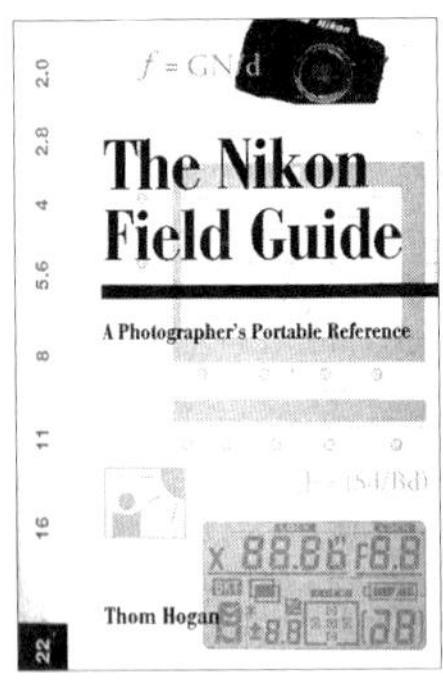

An all-in-one guide for Nikon photographers! Complete, compact, and designed for use in the field, this book provides quick answers to common and unusual questions regarding exposure, equipment, and shooting techniques.

Softbound,
5 x 7-1/2", 256 pages
U.S. List Price $19.95